INVENTIONS AND DISCOVERY

JAKE BURTON CARPENTER
AND THE
SNOWBOARD

by Michael O'Hearn

illustrated by Ron Frenz
and Charles Barnett III

Consultant:
Lee Crane
TransWorld Media
Oceanside, California

Capstone
press®

Mankato, Minnesota

Graphic Library is published by Capstone Press,
151 Good Counsel Drive, P.O. Box 669, Mankato, Minnesota 56002.
www.capstonepress.com

Printed in the United States of America

1 2 3 4 5 6 11 10 09 08 07 06

Library of Congress Cataloging-in-Publication Data
O'Hearn, Michael, 1972–
Jake Burton Carpenter and the snowboard / by Michael O'Hearn; illustrated by Ron Frenz and Charles Barnett III.
p. cm.—(Graphic library. Inventions and discovery)
Includes bibliographical references and index.
ISBN-13: 978-0-7368-6481-7 (hardcover)
ISBN-10: 0-7368-6481-4 (hardcover)
ISBN-13: 978-0-7368-9643-6 (softcover pbk.)
ISBN-10: 0-7368-9643-0 (softcover pbk.)
1. Carpenter, Jake Burton—Juvenile literature. 2. Snowboarders—United States—Biography—Juvenile literature. 3. Snowboards—Design and construction—Juvenile literature. I. Frenz, Ron. II. Barnett, Charles, III. III. Title. IV. Series.
GV857.S57O44 2007
796.93'9092—dc22 2006008176

Summary: In graphic novel format, tells the story of Jake Burton Carpenter and the evolution of the snowboard and the sport of snowboarding.

Design
Jason Knudson

Colorist
Ben Hunzeker

Editor
Donald Lemke

TABLE OF CONTENTS

Chapter 1
Snurfing USA

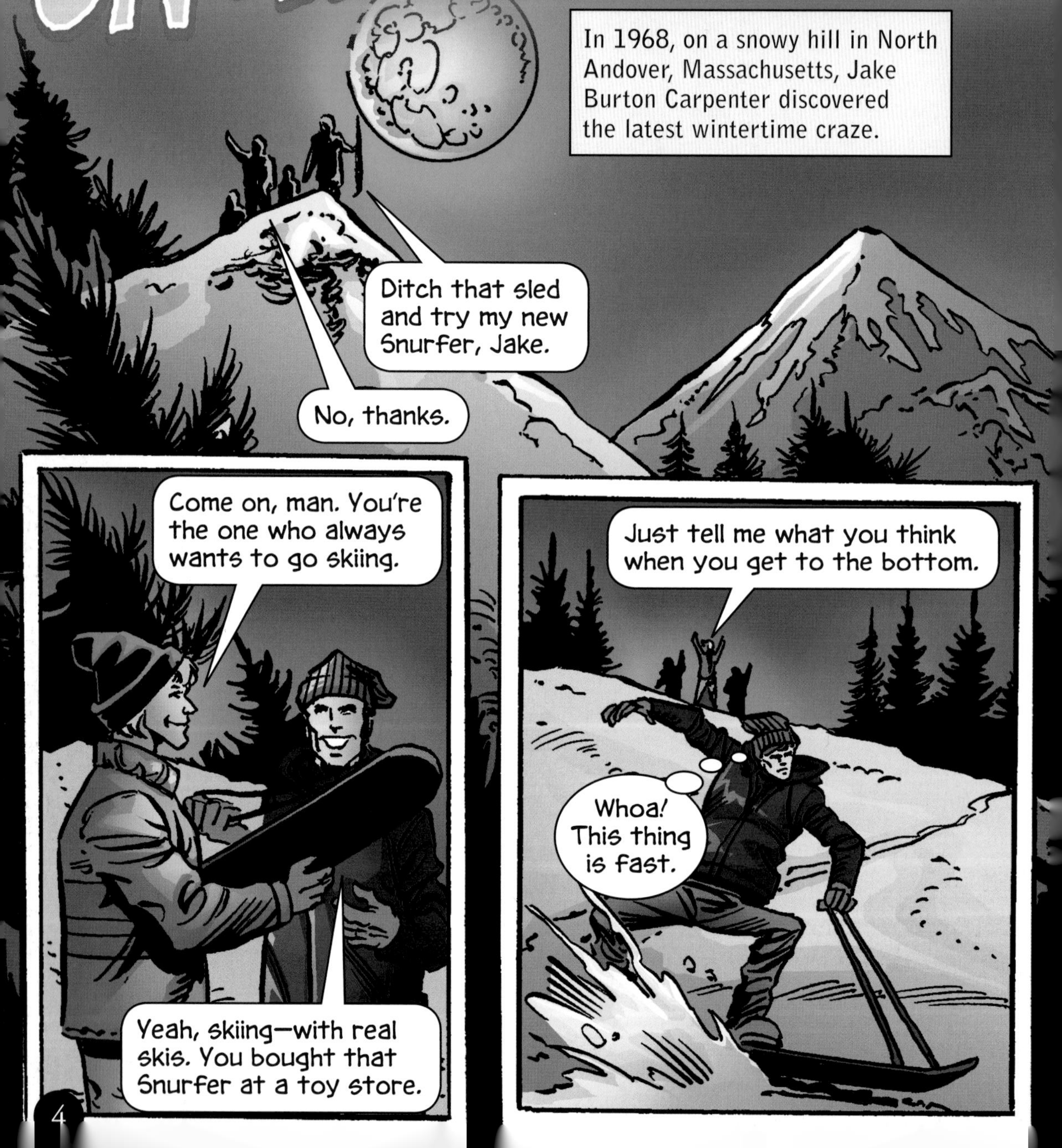

In 1968, on a snowy hill in North Andover, Massachusetts, Jake Burton Carpenter discovered the latest wintertime craze.
Ditch that sled and try my new Snurfer, Jake.
No, thanks.
Come on, man. You're the one who always wants to go skiing.
Yeah, skiing—with real skis. You bought that Snurfer at a toy store.
Just tell me what you think when you get to the bottom.
Whoa! This thing is fast.

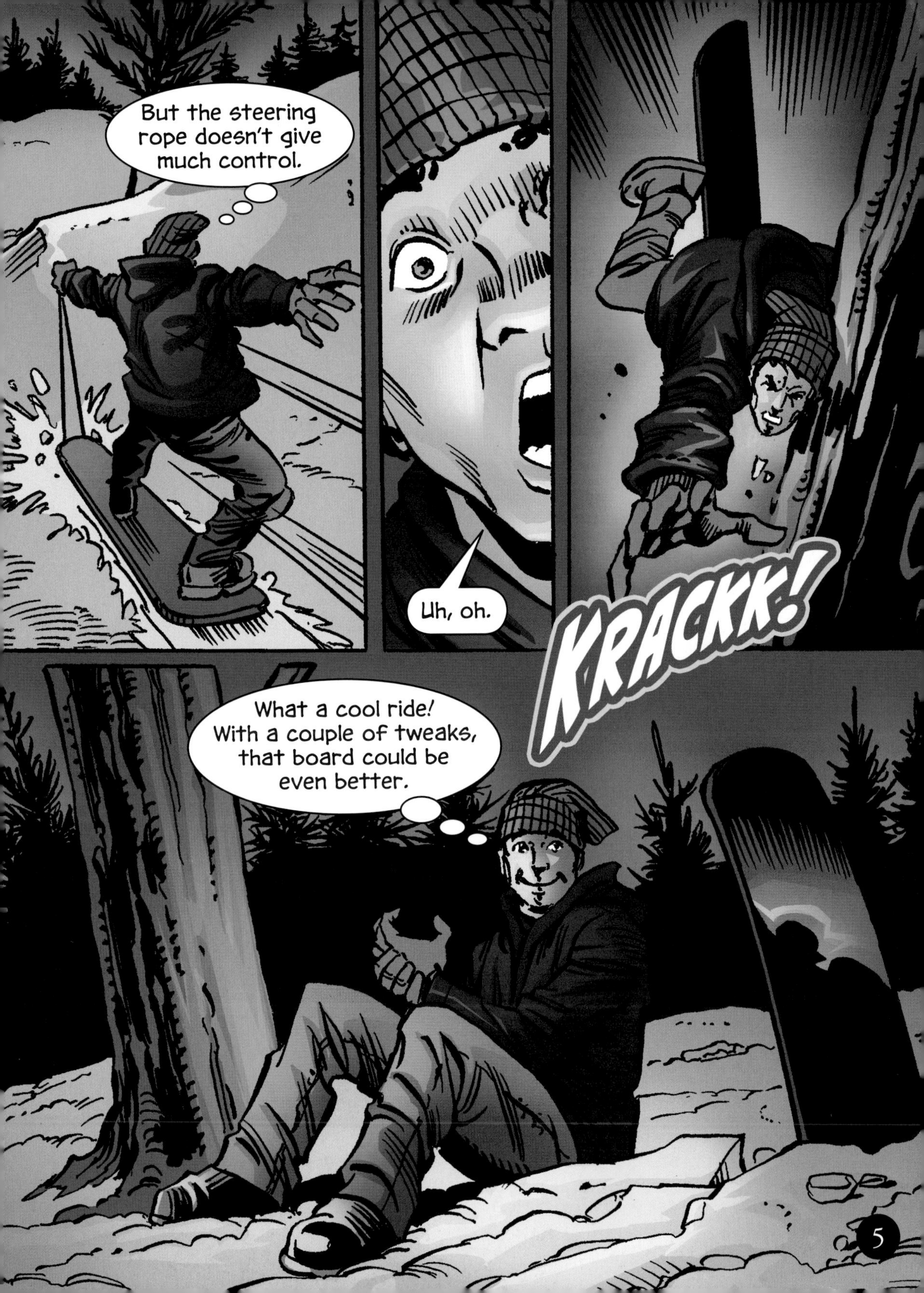
But the steering rope doesn't give much control.
Uh, oh.
KRACKK!
What a cool ride! With a couple of tweaks, that board could be even better.

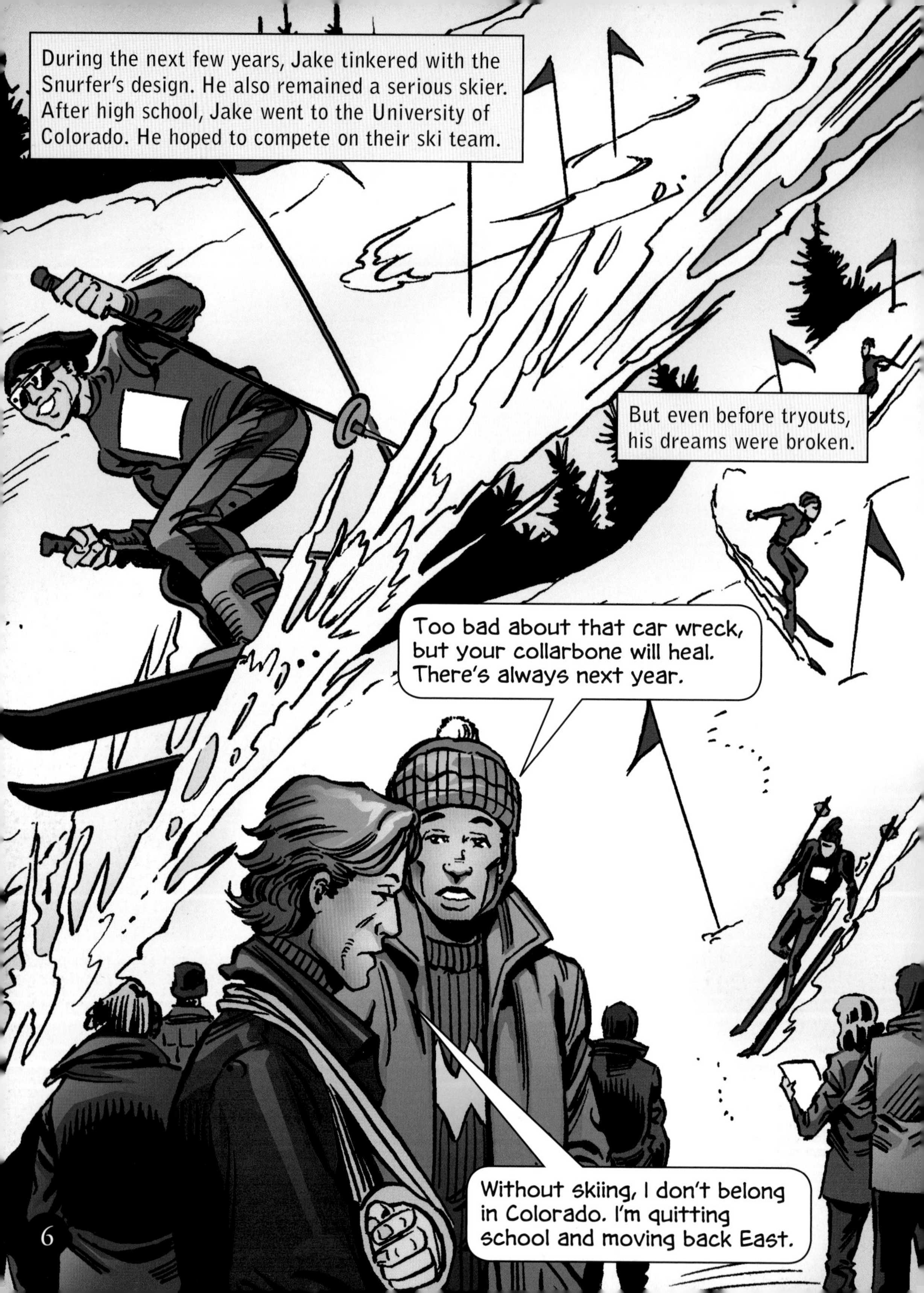
During the next few years, Jake tinkered with the Snurfer's design. He also remained a serious skier. After high school, Jake went to the University of Colorado. He hoped to compete on their ski team.
But even before tryouts, his dreams were broken.
Too bad about that car wreck, but your collarbone will heal. There's always next year.
Without skiing, I don't belong in Colorado. I'm quitting school and moving back East.

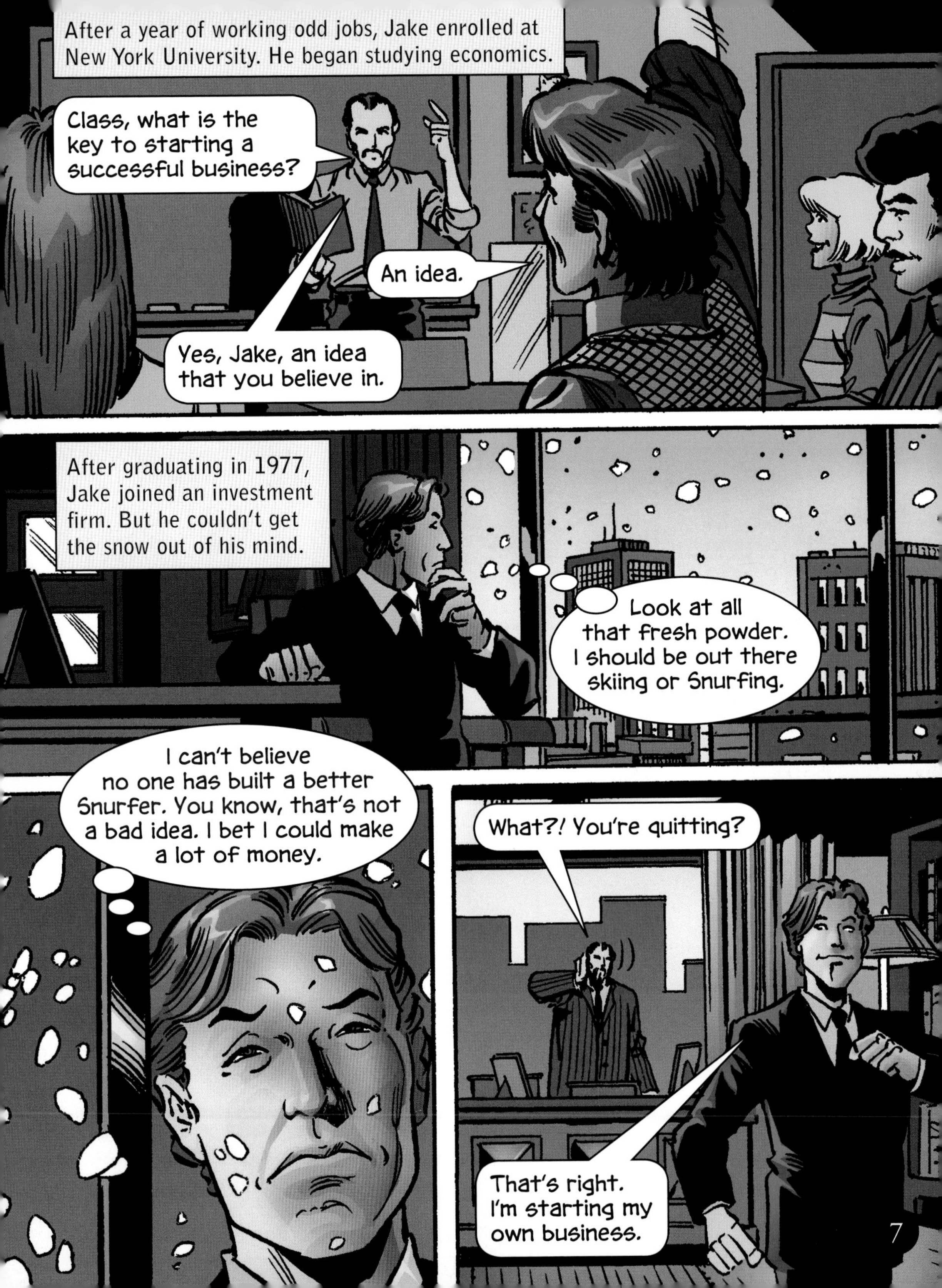
After a year of working odd jobs, Jake enrolled at New York University. He began studying economics.
Class, what is the key to starting a successful business?
An idea.
Yes, Jake, an idea that you believe in.
After graduating in 1977, Jake joined an investment firm. But he couldn't get the snow out of his mind.
Look at all that fresh powder. I should be out there skiing or Snurfing.
I can't believe no one has built a better Snurfer. You know, that's not a bad idea. I bet I could make a lot of money.
What?! You're quitting?
That's right. I'm starting my own business.

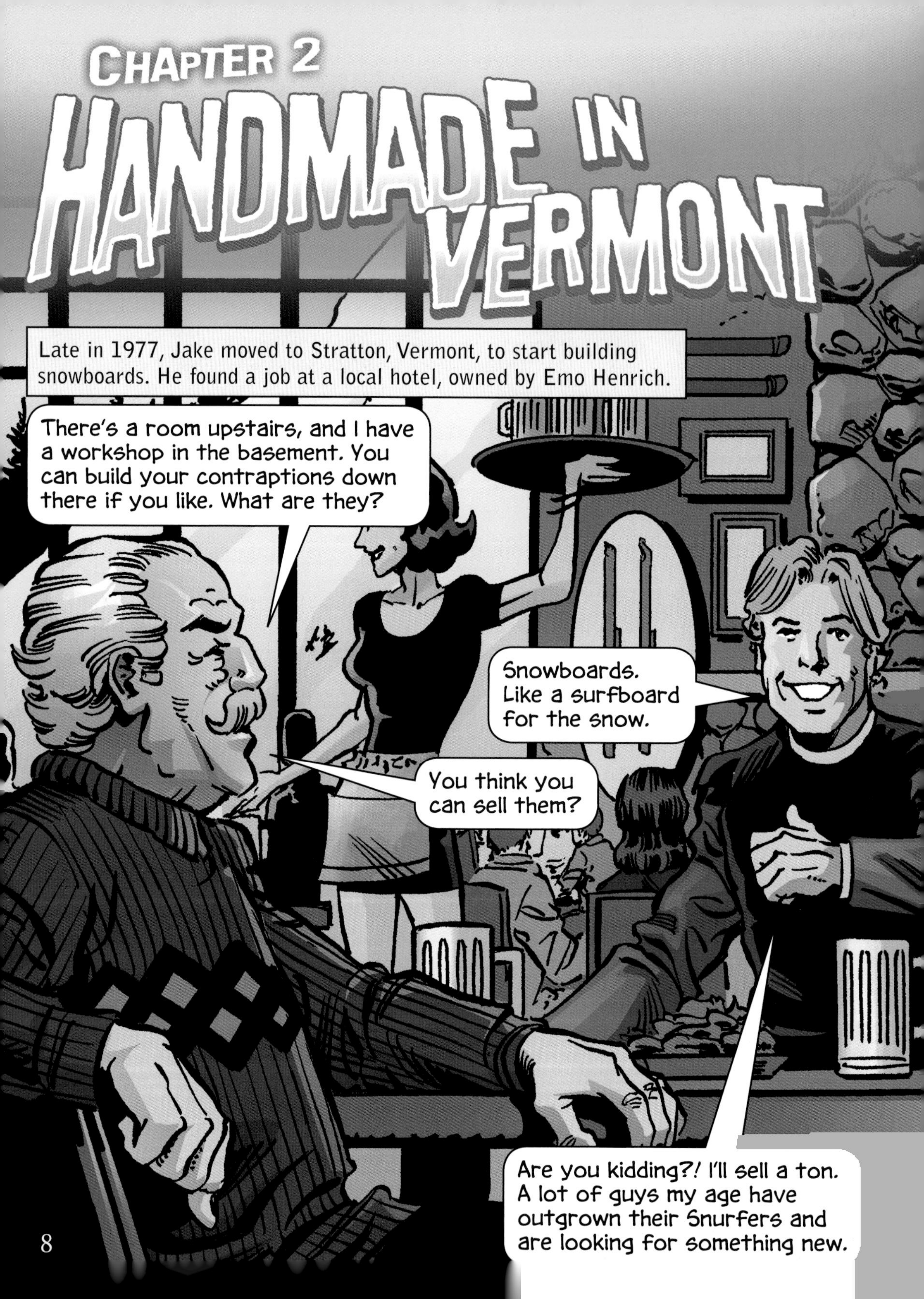
CHAPTER 2
HANDMADE IN VERMONT
Late in 1977, Jake moved to Stratton, Vermont, to start building snowboards. He found a job at a local hotel, owned by Emo Henrich.
There's a room upstairs, and I have a workshop in the basement. You can build your contraptions down there if you like. What are they?
Snowboards. Like a surfboard for the snow.
You think you can sell them?
Are you kidding?! I'll sell a ton. A lot of guys my age have outgrown their Snurfers and are looking for something new.

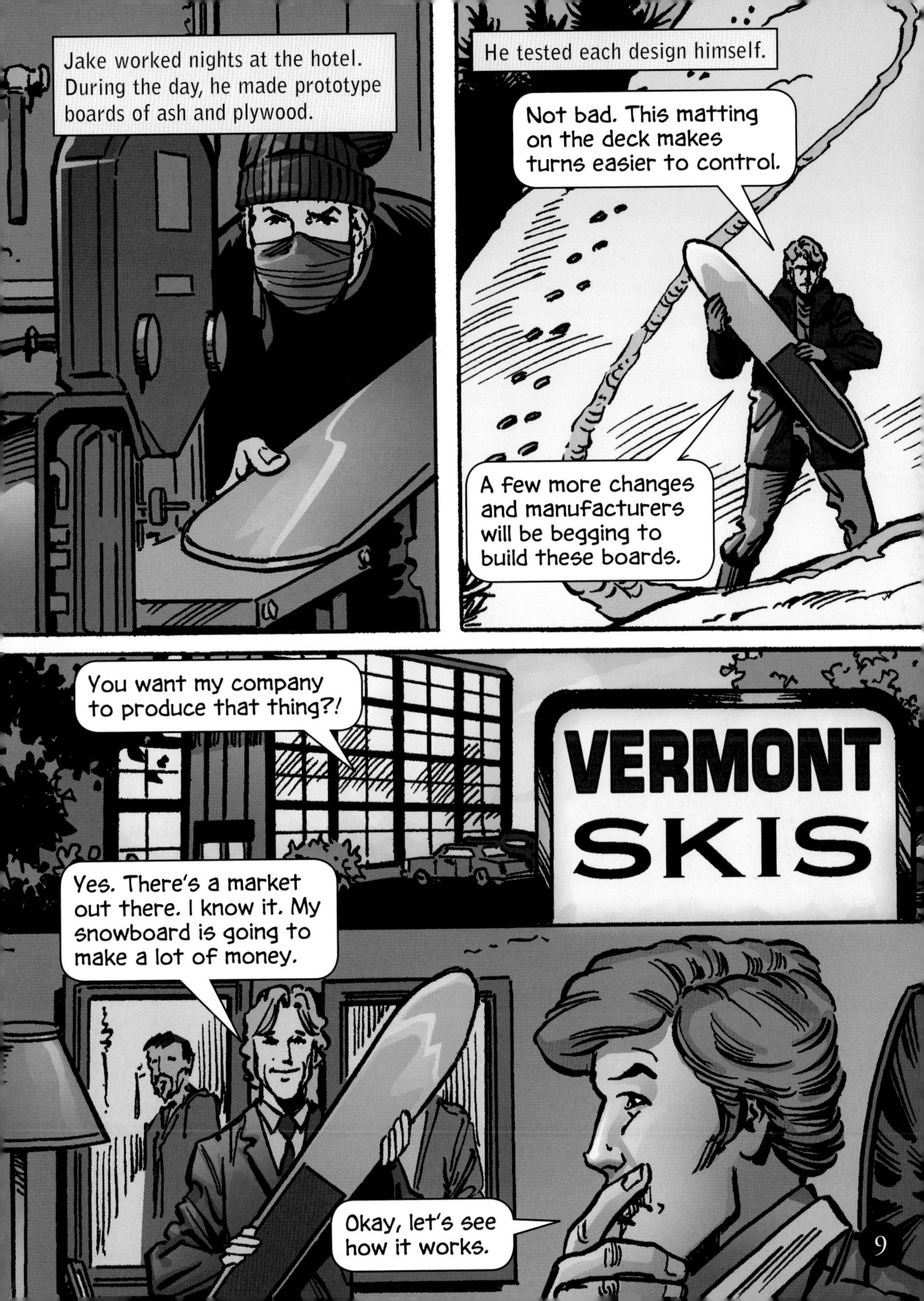
Jake worked nights at the hotel. During the day, he made prototype boards of ash and plywood.
He tested each design himself.
Not bad. This matting on the deck makes turns easier to control.
A few more changes and manufacturers will be begging to build these boards.
You want my company to produce that thing?!
VERMONT SKIS
Yes. There's a market out there. I know it. My snowboard is going to make a lot of money.
Okay, let's see how it works.

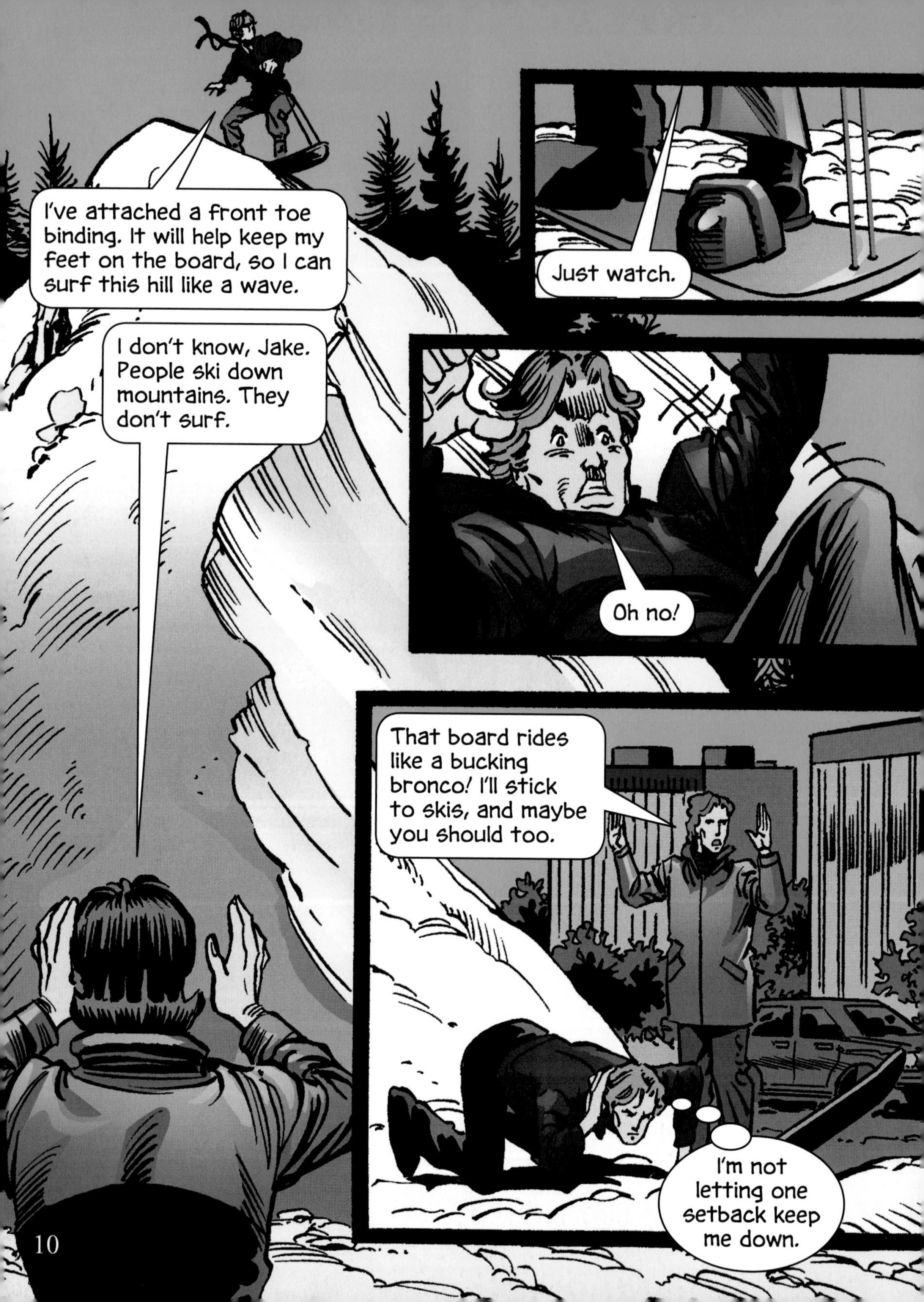
I've attached a front toe binding. It will help keep my feet on the board, so I can surf this hill like a wave.
I don't know, Jake. People ski down mountains. They don't surf.
Just watch.
Oh no!
That board rides like a bucking bronco! I'll stick to skis, and maybe you should too.
I'm not letting one setback keep me down.

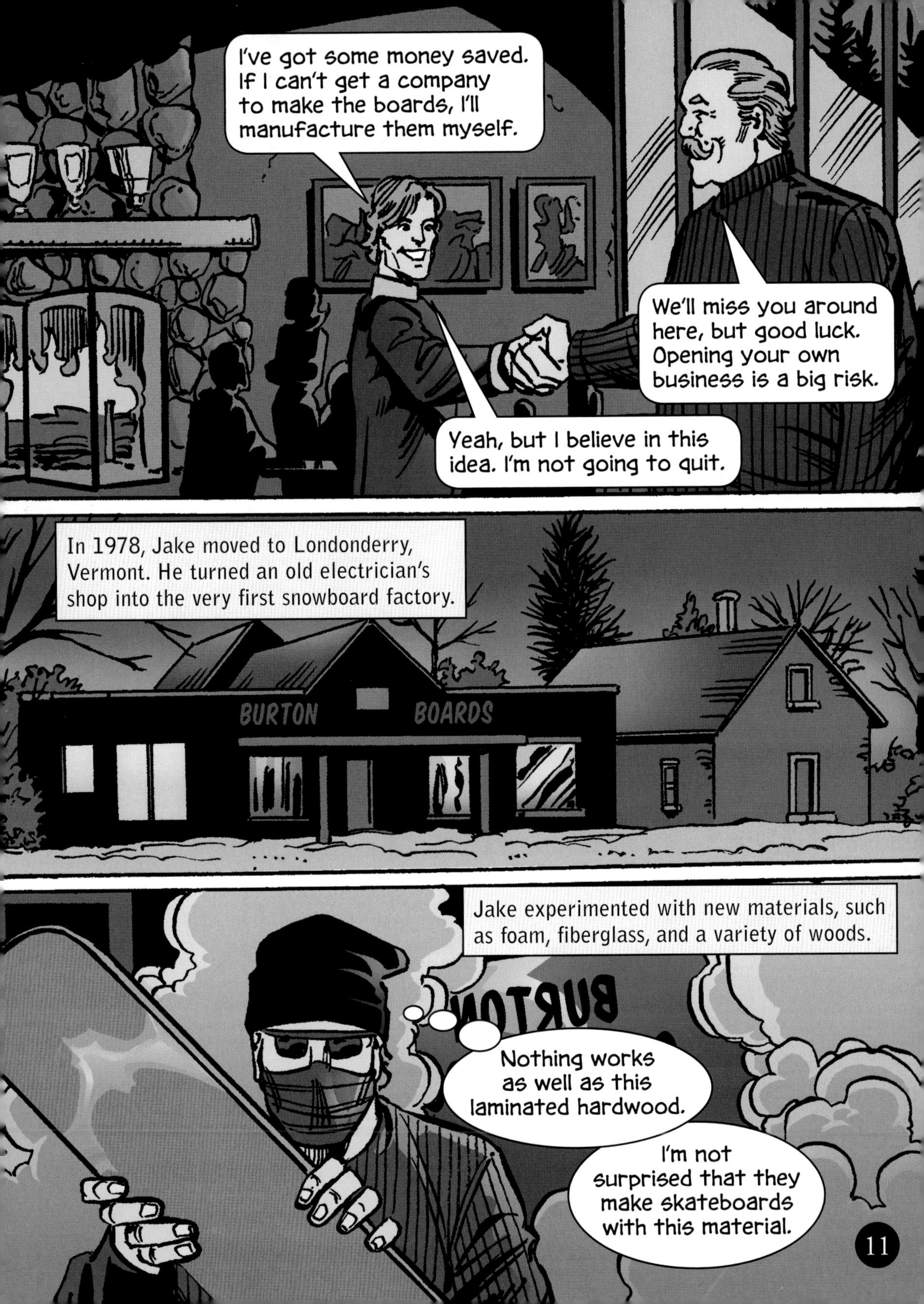
I've got some money saved. If I can't get a company to make the boards, I'll manufacture them myself.
We'll miss you around here, but good luck. Opening your own business is a big risk.
Yeah, but I believe in this idea. I'm not going to quit.
In 1978, Jake moved to Londonderry, Vermont. He turned an old electrician's shop into the very first snowboard factory.
BURTON BOARDS
Jake experimented with new materials, such as foam, fiberglass, and a variety of woods.
BURTON
Nothing works as well as this laminated hardwood.
I'm not surprised that they make skateboards with this material.

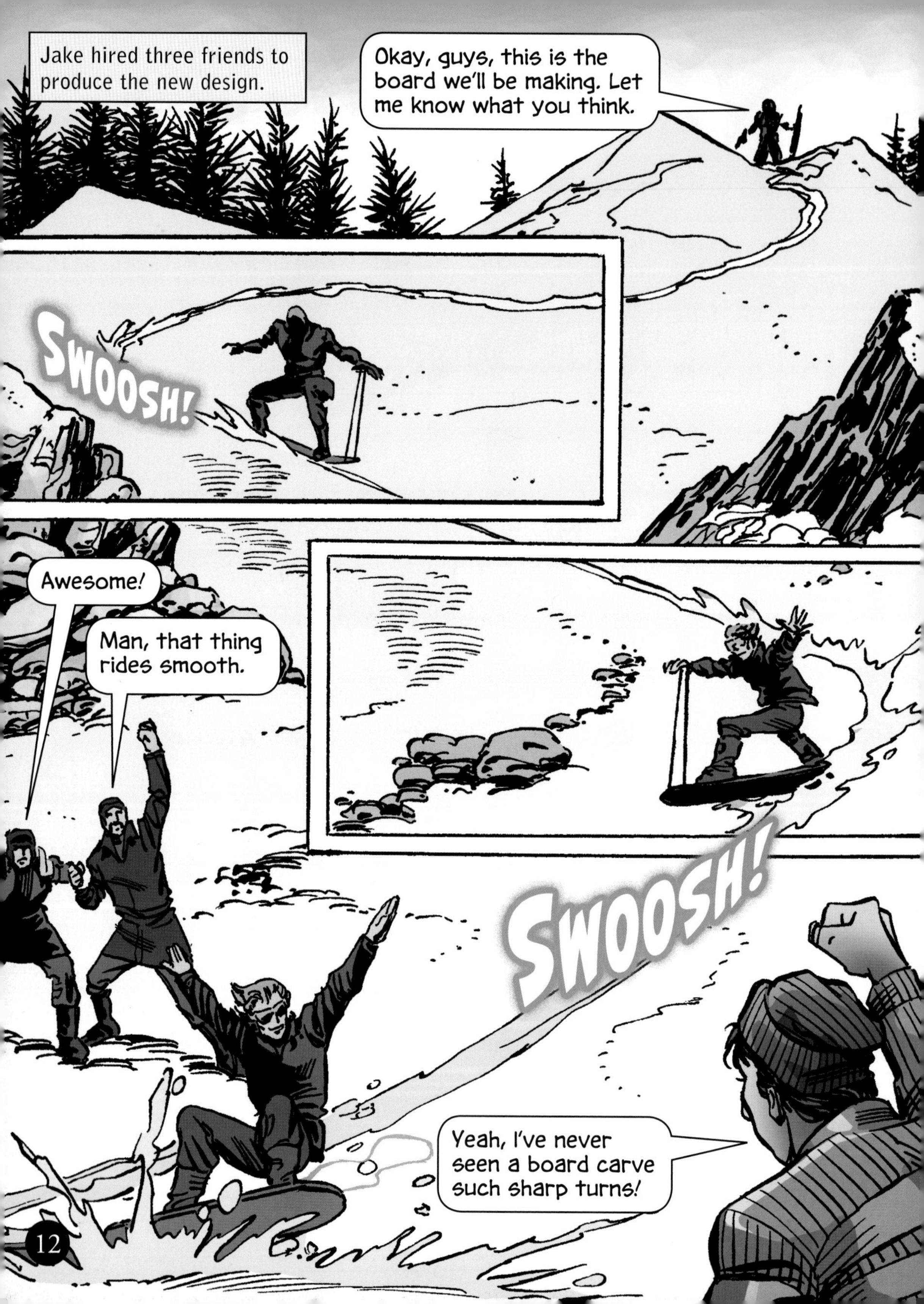
Jake hired three friends to produce the new design.
Okay, guys, this is the board we'll be making. Let me know what you think.
SWOOSH!
Awesome!
Man, that thing rides smooth.
SWOOSH!
Yeah, I've never seen a board carve such sharp turns!

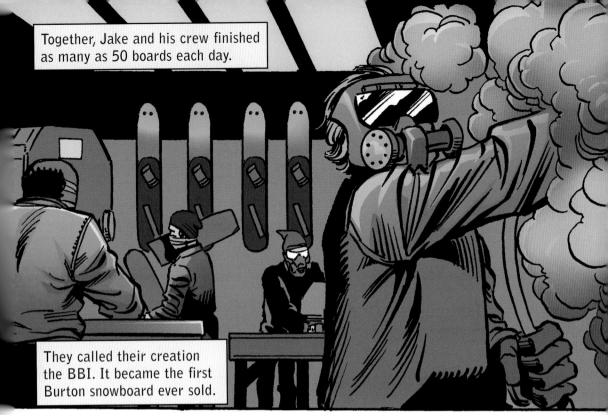

Together, Jake and his crew finished as many as 50 boards each day.

They called their creation the BBI. It became the first Burton snowboard ever sold.

Perfect. This front binding will make it more controllable than the Snurfer.

And these tail fins will really rip through the turns.

Now I just have to sell them.

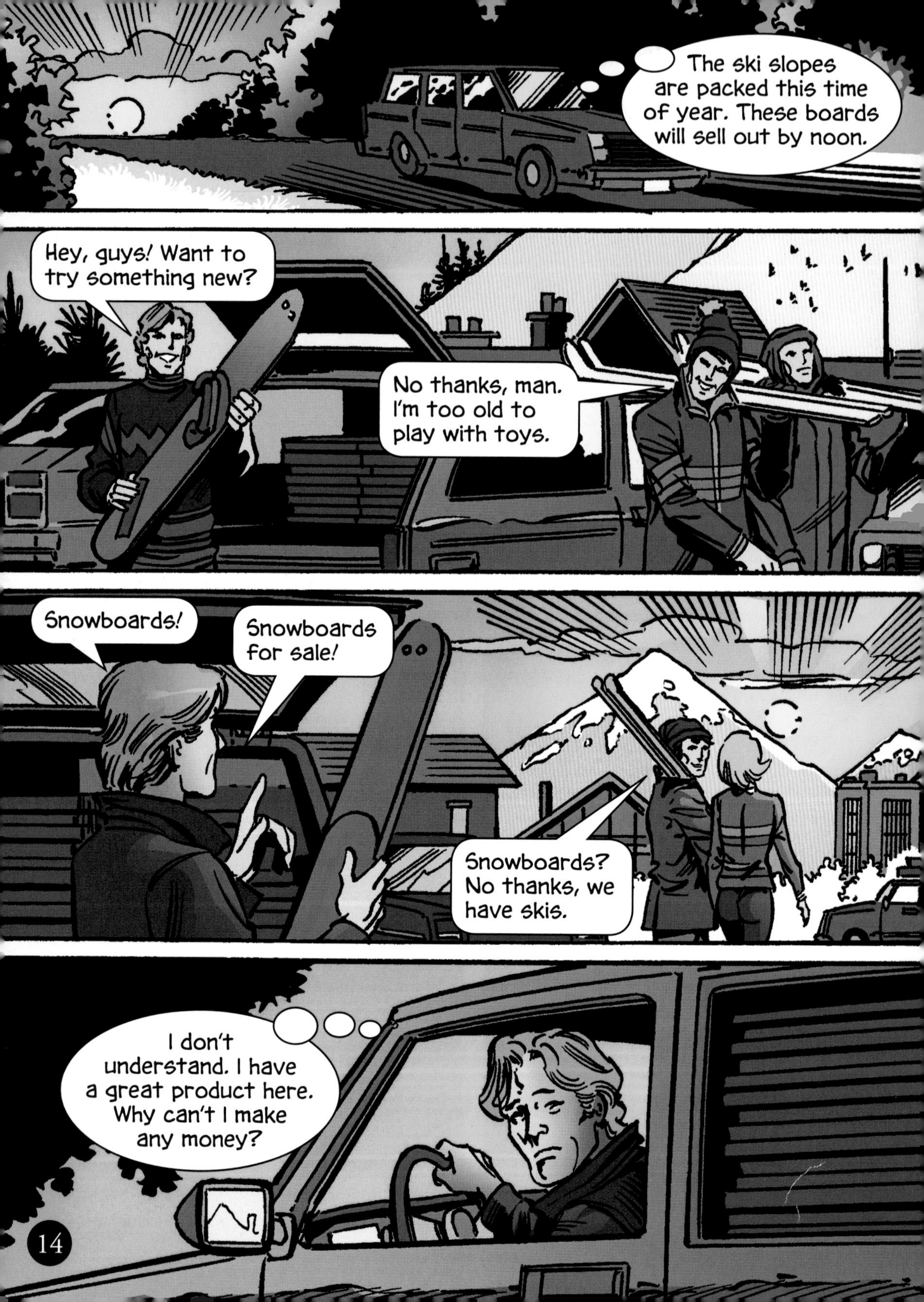
The ski slopes are packed this time of year. These boards will sell out by noon.
Hey, guys! Want to try something new?
No thanks, man. I'm too old to play with toys.
Snowboards!
Snowboards for sale!
Snowboards? No thanks, we have skis.
I don't understand. I have a great product here. Why can't I make any money?

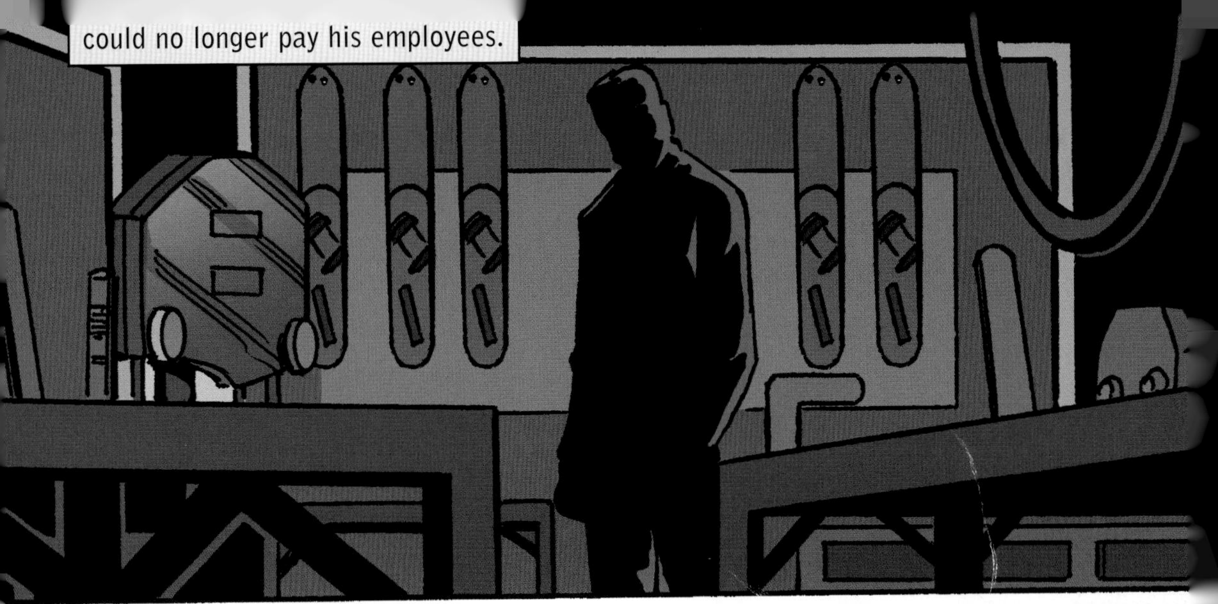
could no longer pay his employees.

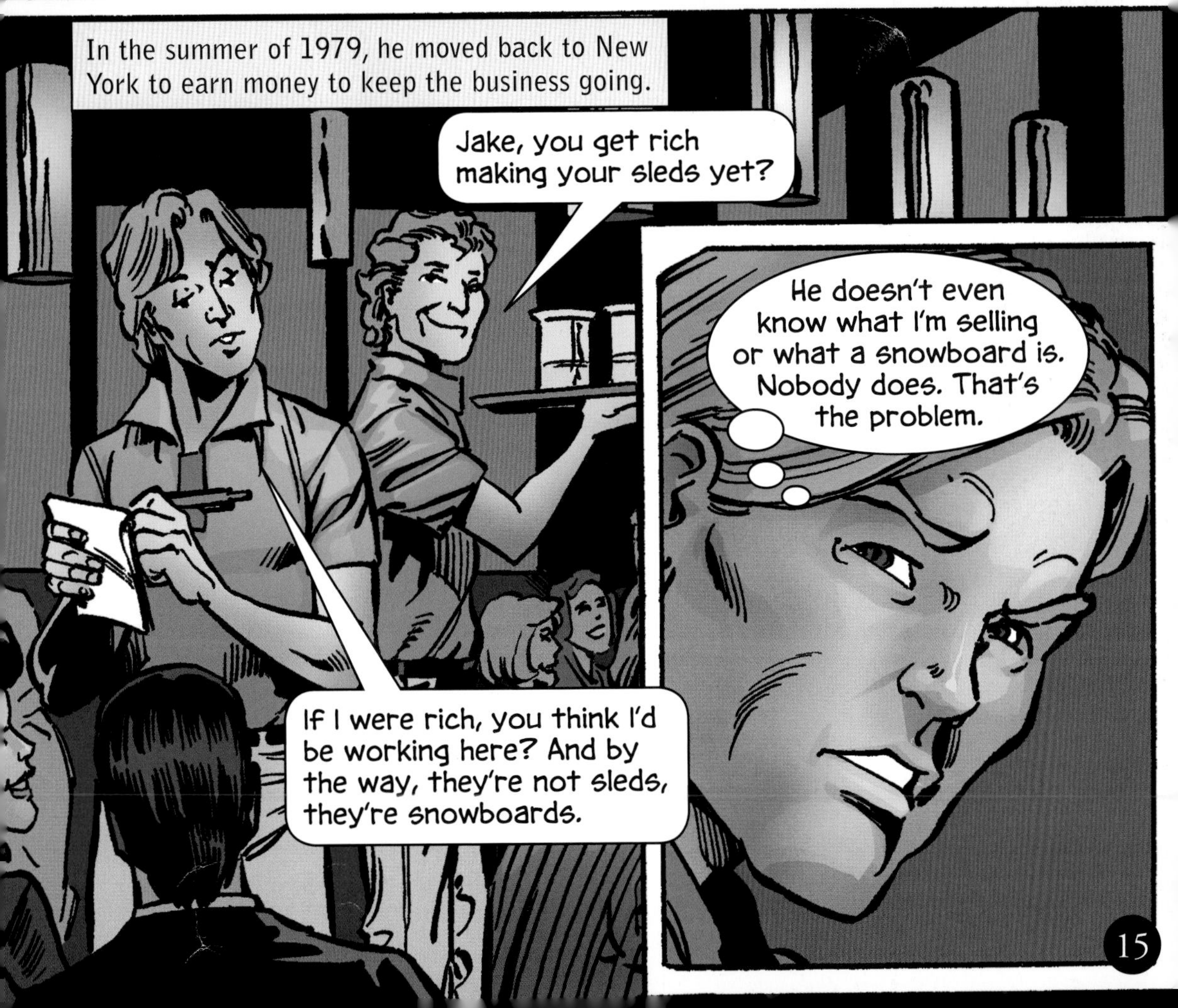
In the summer of 1979, he moved back to New York to earn money to keep the business going.
Jake, you get rich making your sleds yet?
If I were rich, you think I'd be working here? And by the way, they're not sleds, they're snowboards.
He doesn't even know what I'm selling or what a snowboard is. Nobody does. That's the problem.

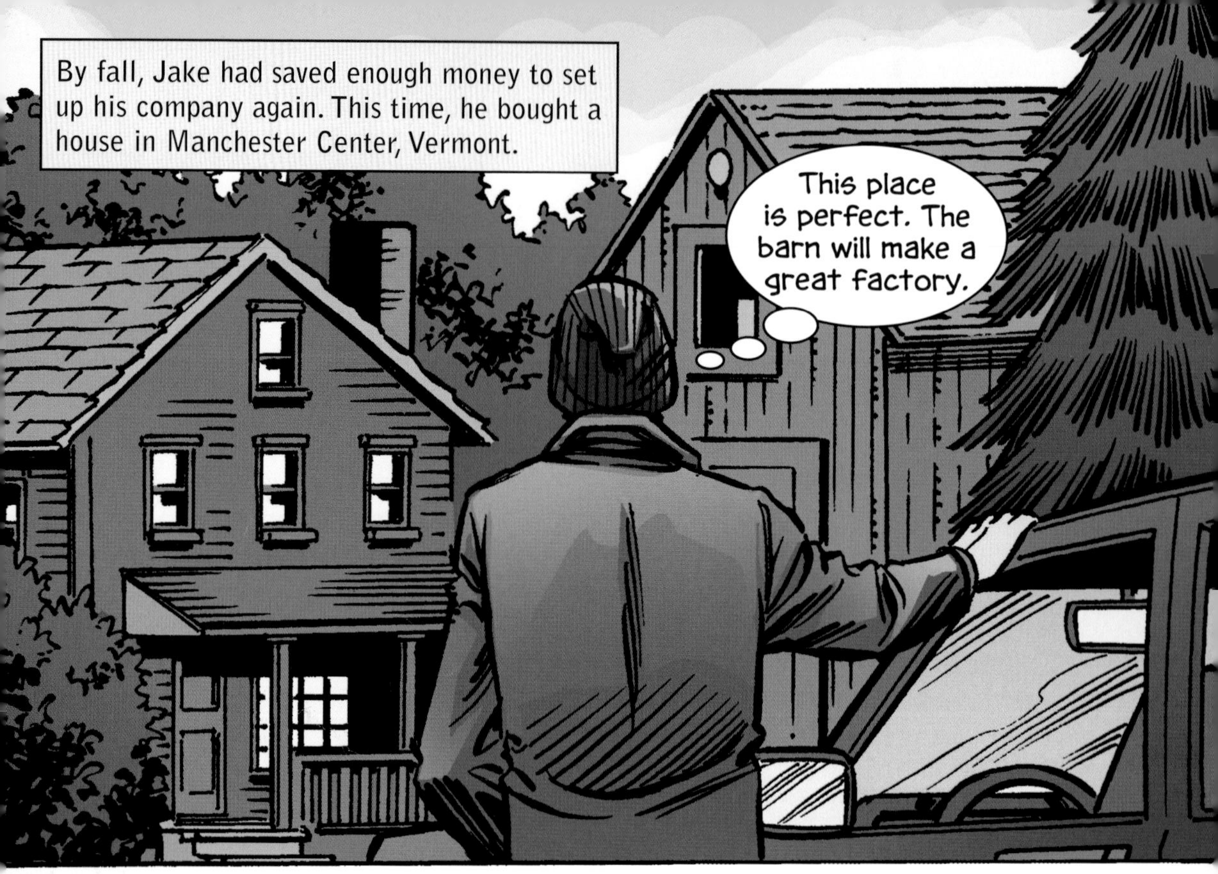
By fall, Jake had saved enough money to set up his company again. This time, he bought a house in Manchester Center, Vermont.
This place is perfect. The barn will make a great factory.

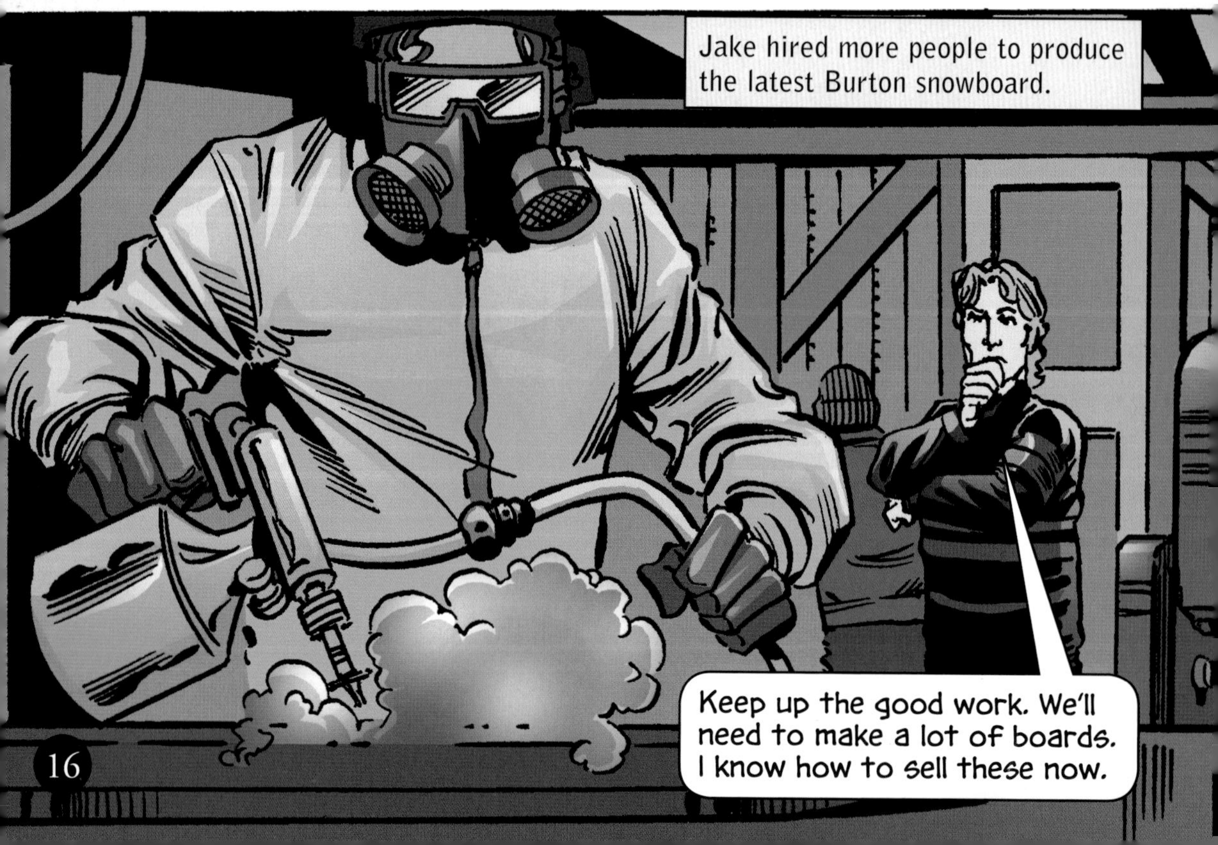
Jake hired more people to produce the latest Burton snowboard.
Keep up the good work. We'll need to make a lot of boards. I know how to sell these now.

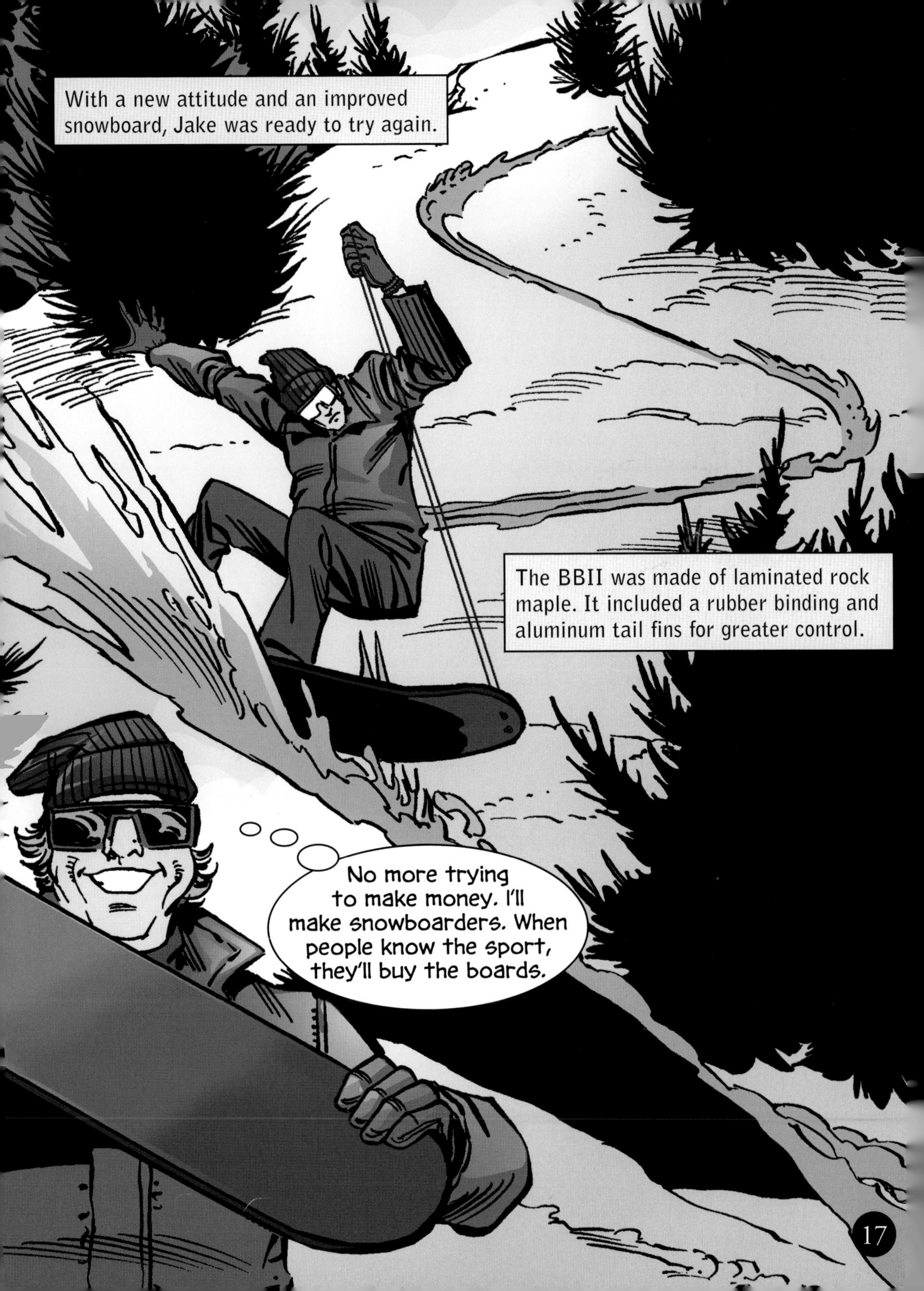
With a new attitude and an improved snowboard, Jake was ready to try again.
The BBII was made of laminated rock maple. It included a rubber binding and aluminum tail fins for greater control.
No more trying to make money. I'll make snowboarders. When people know the sport, they'll buy the boards.

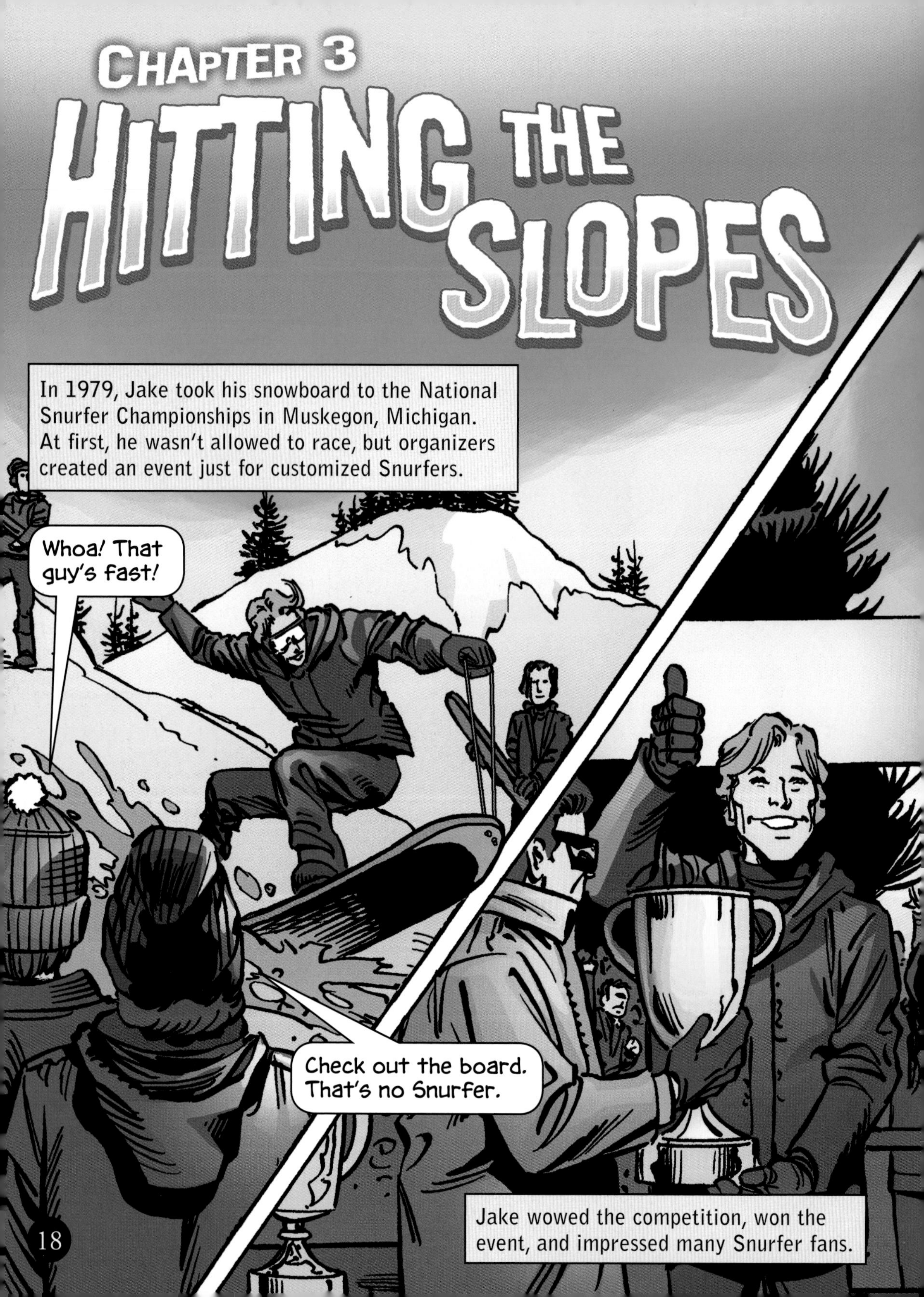

CHAPTER 3
HITTING THE SLOPES

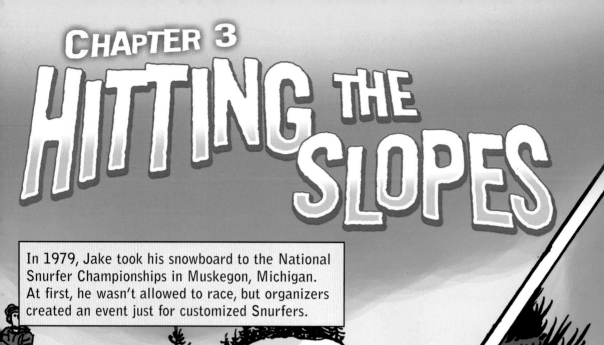

In 1979, Jake took his snowboard to the National Snurfer Championships in Muskegon, Michigan. At first, he wasn't allowed to race, but organizers created an event just for customized Snurfers.

Whoa! That guy's fast!

Check out the board. That's no Snurfer.

Jake wowed the competition, won the event, and impressed many Snurfer fans.

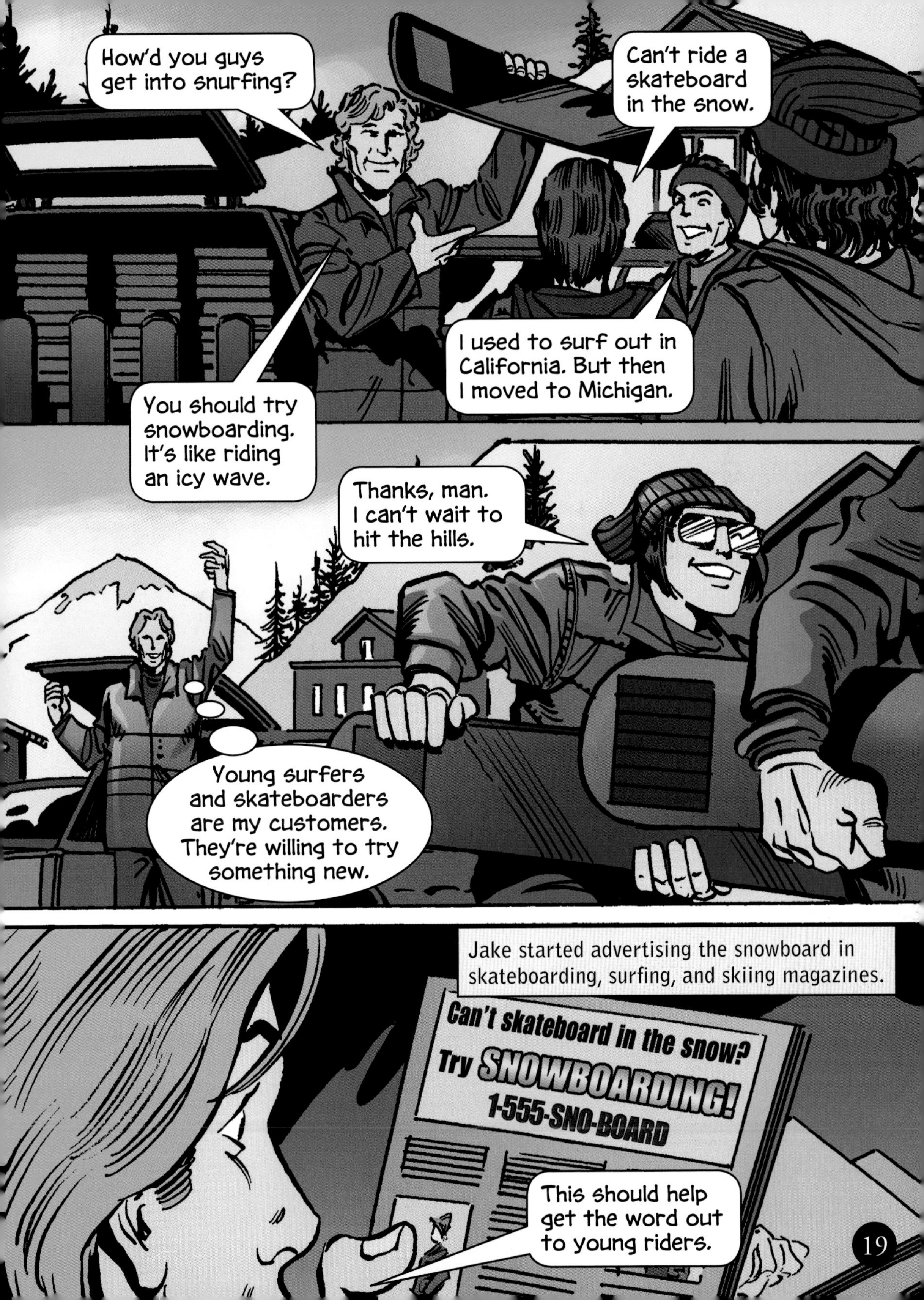
How'd you guys get into snurfing?
Can't ride a skateboard in the snow.
I used to surf out in California. But then I moved to Michigan.
You should try snowboarding. It's like riding an icy wave.
Thanks, man. I can't wait to hit the hills.
Young surfers and skateboarders are my customers. They're willing to try something new.
Jake started advertising the snowboard in skateboarding, surfing, and skiing magazines.
Can't skateboard in the snow?
Try SNOWBOARDING!
1-555-SNO-BOARD
This should help get the word out to young riders.

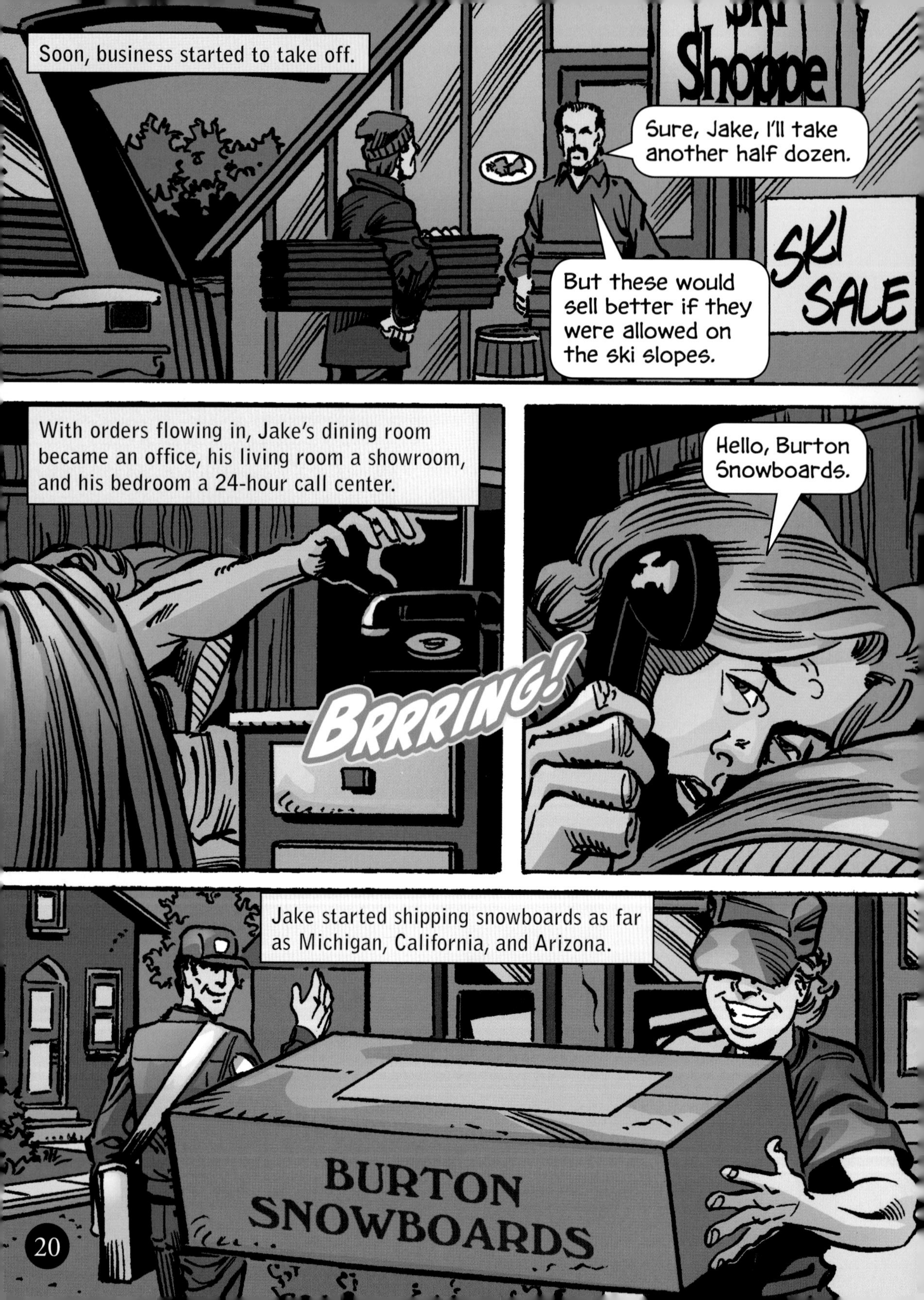
Soon, business started to take off.
Shoppe
Sure, Jake, I'll take another half dozen.
But these would sell better if they were allowed on the ski slopes.
SKI SALE
With orders flowing in, Jake's dining room became an office, his living room a showroom, and his bedroom a 24-hour call center.
BRRRING!
Hello, Burton Snowboards.
Jake started shipping snowboards as far as Michigan, California, and Arizona.
BURTON SNOWBOARDS

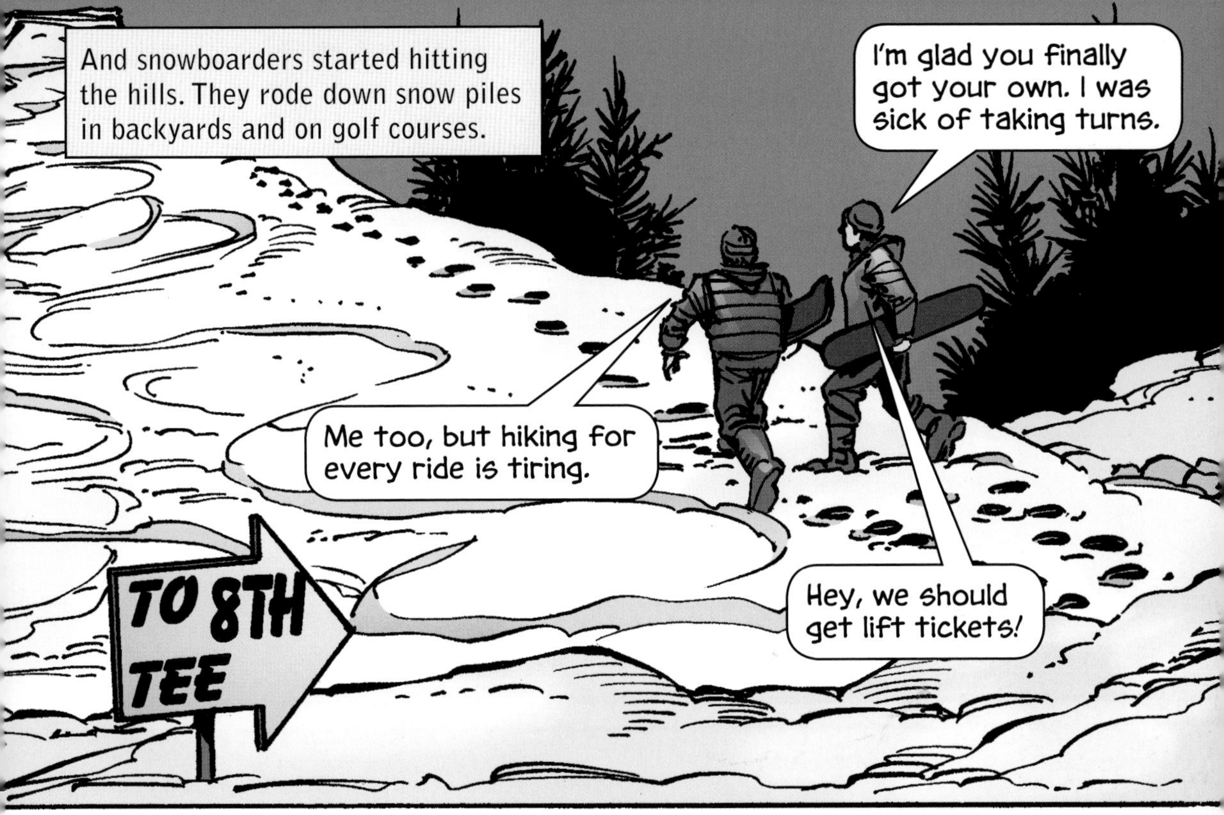
And snowboarders started hitting the hills. They rode down snow piles in backyards and on golf courses.
I'm glad you finally got your own. I was sick of taking turns.
Me too, but hiking for every ride is tiring.
TO 8TH TEE
Hey, we should get lift tickets!

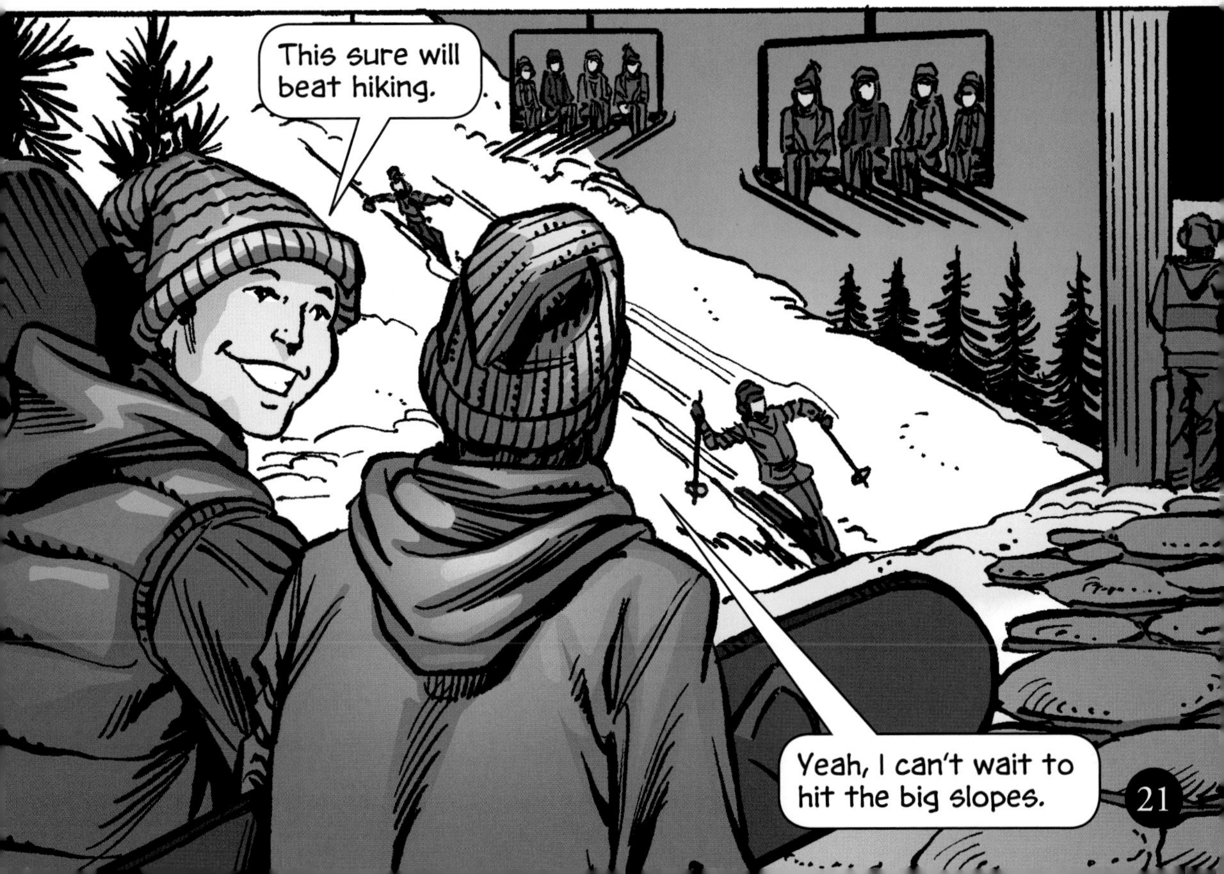
This sure will beat hiking.
Yeah, I can't wait to hit the big slopes.

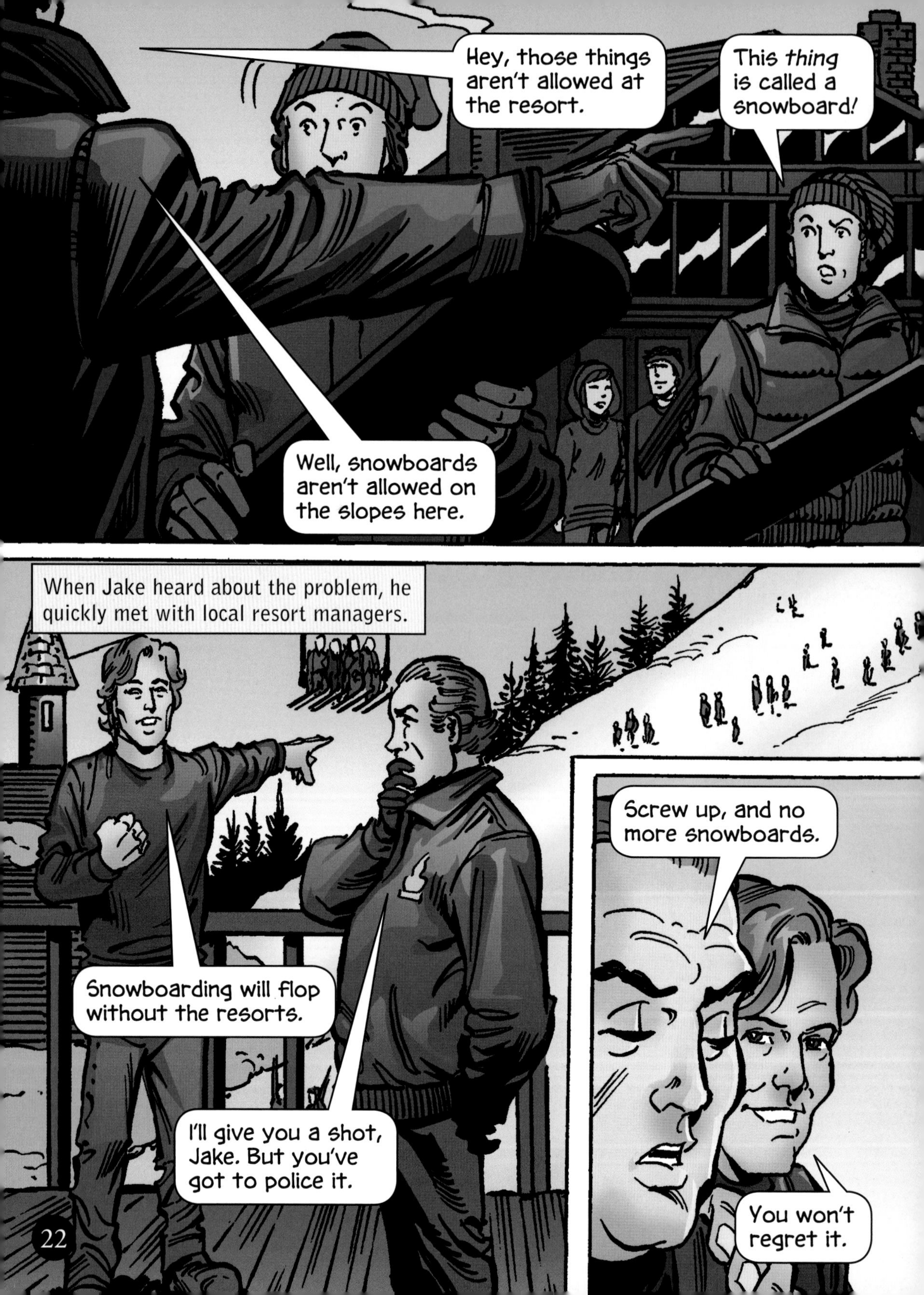
Hey, those things aren't allowed at the resort.
This *thing* is called a snowboard!
Well, snowboards aren't allowed on the slopes here.
When Jake heard about the problem, he quickly met with local resort managers.
Snowboarding will flop without the resorts.
I'll give you a shot, Jake. But you've got to police it.
Screw up, and no more snowboards.
You won't regret it.

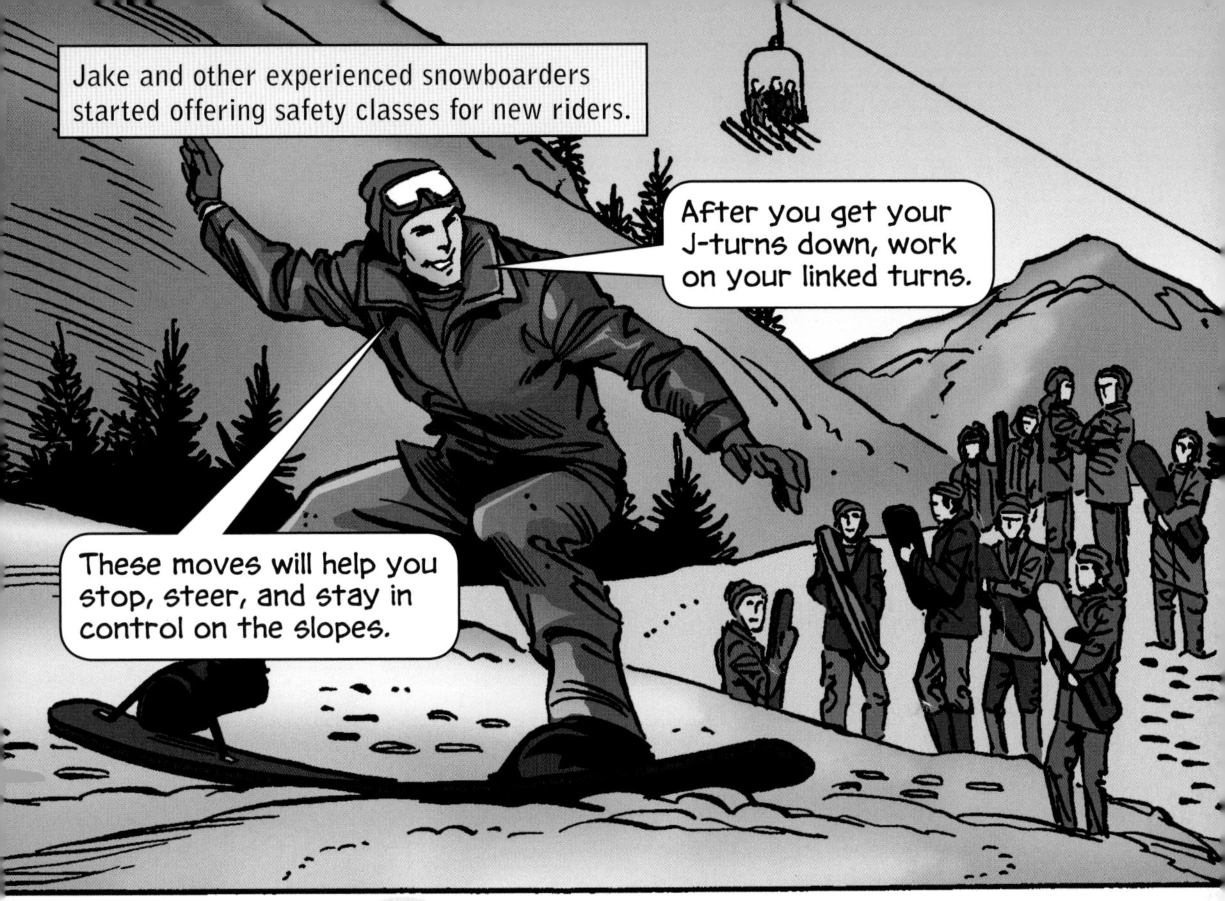
Jake and other experienced snowboarders started offering safety classes for new riders.
After you get your J-turns down, work on your linked turns.
These moves will help you stop, steer, and stay in control on the slopes.

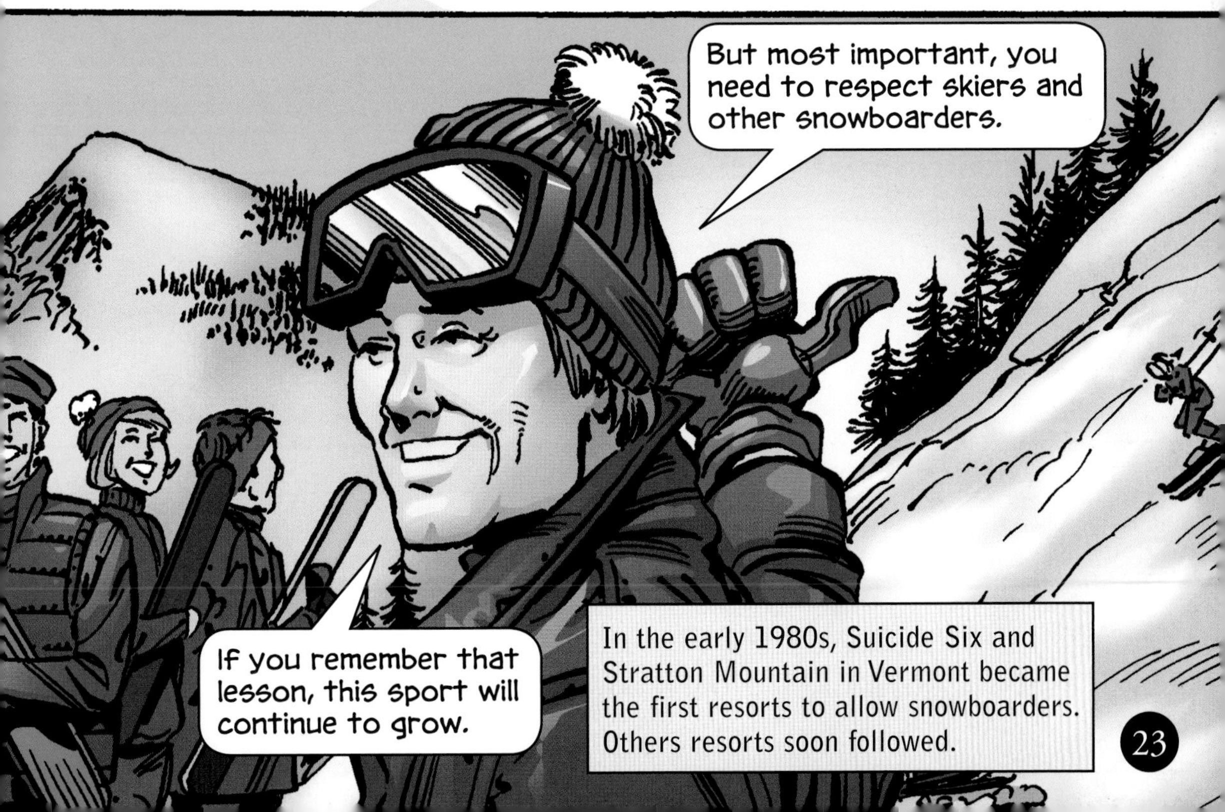
But most important, you need to respect skiers and other snowboarders.
If you remember that lesson, this sport will continue to grow.
In the early 1980s, Suicide Six and Stratton Mountain in Vermont became the first resorts to allow snowboarders. Others resorts soon followed.

CHAPTER 4

SNOWBOARDING SCORES BIG

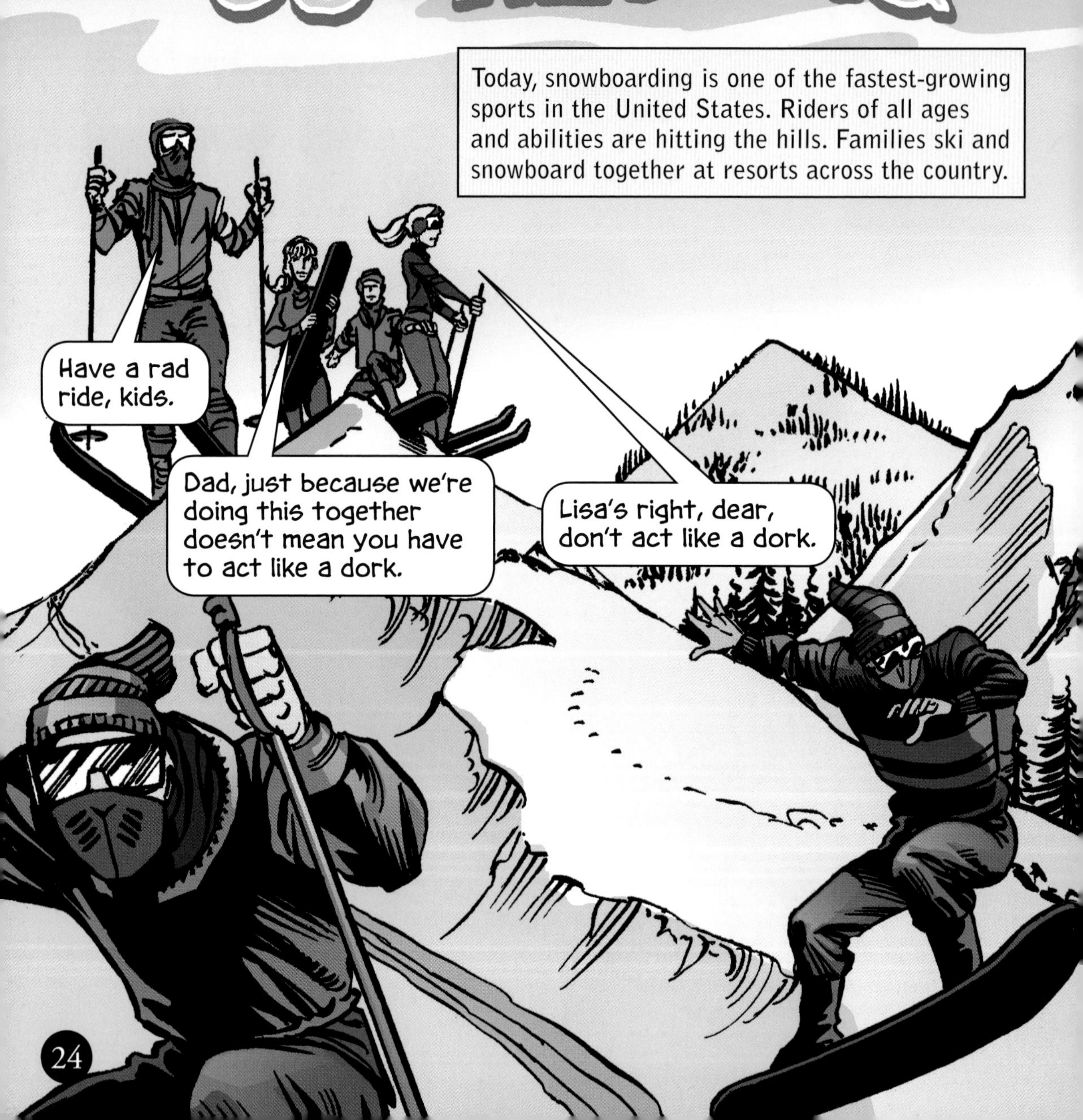
Today, snowboarding is one of the fastest-growing sports in the United States. Riders of all ages and abilities are hitting the hills. Families ski and snowboard together at resorts across the country.
Have a rad ride, kids.
Dad, just because we're doing this together doesn't mean you have to act like a dork.
Lisa's right, dear, don't act like a dork.

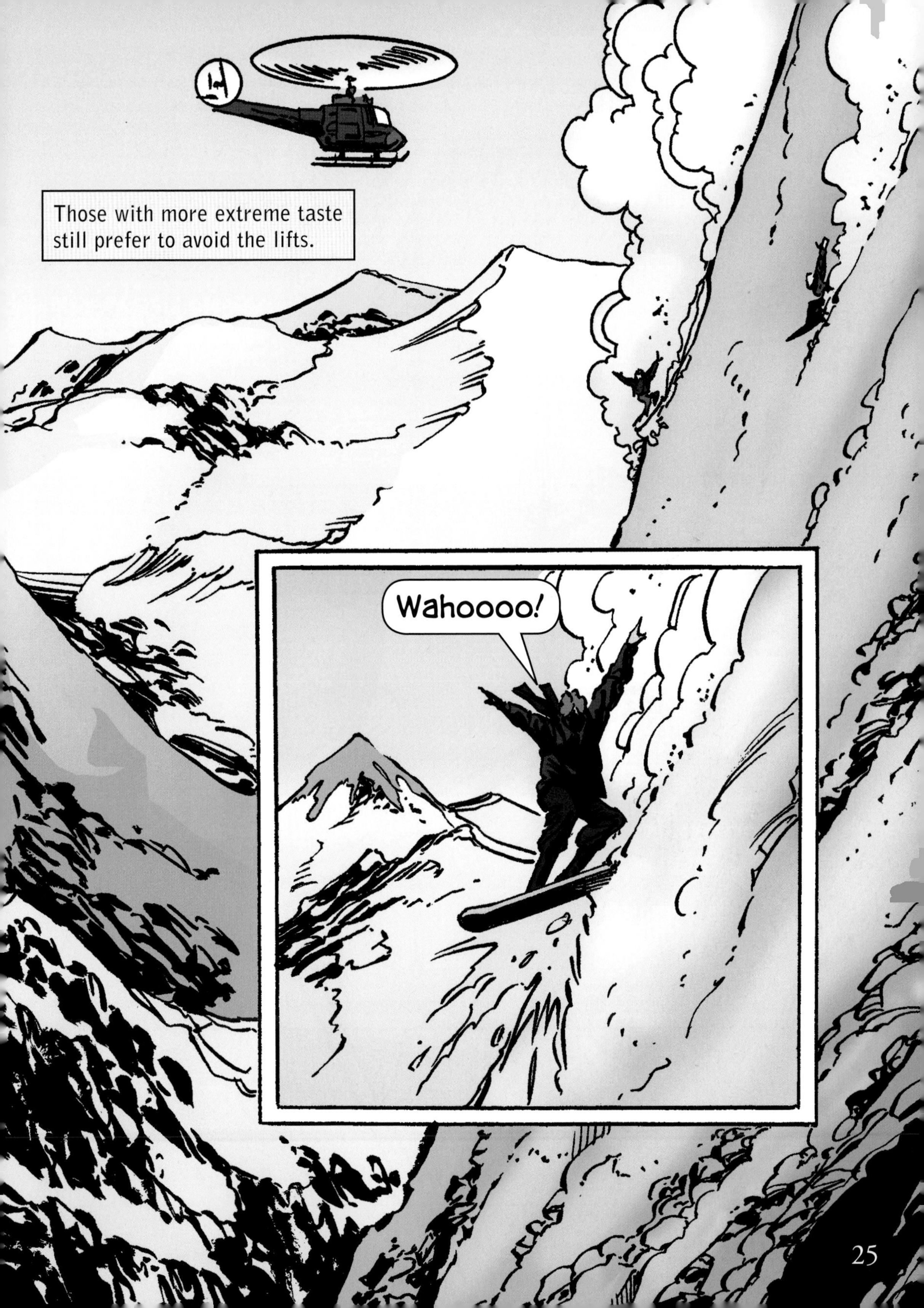
Those with more extreme taste still prefer to avoid the lifts.
Wahoooo!

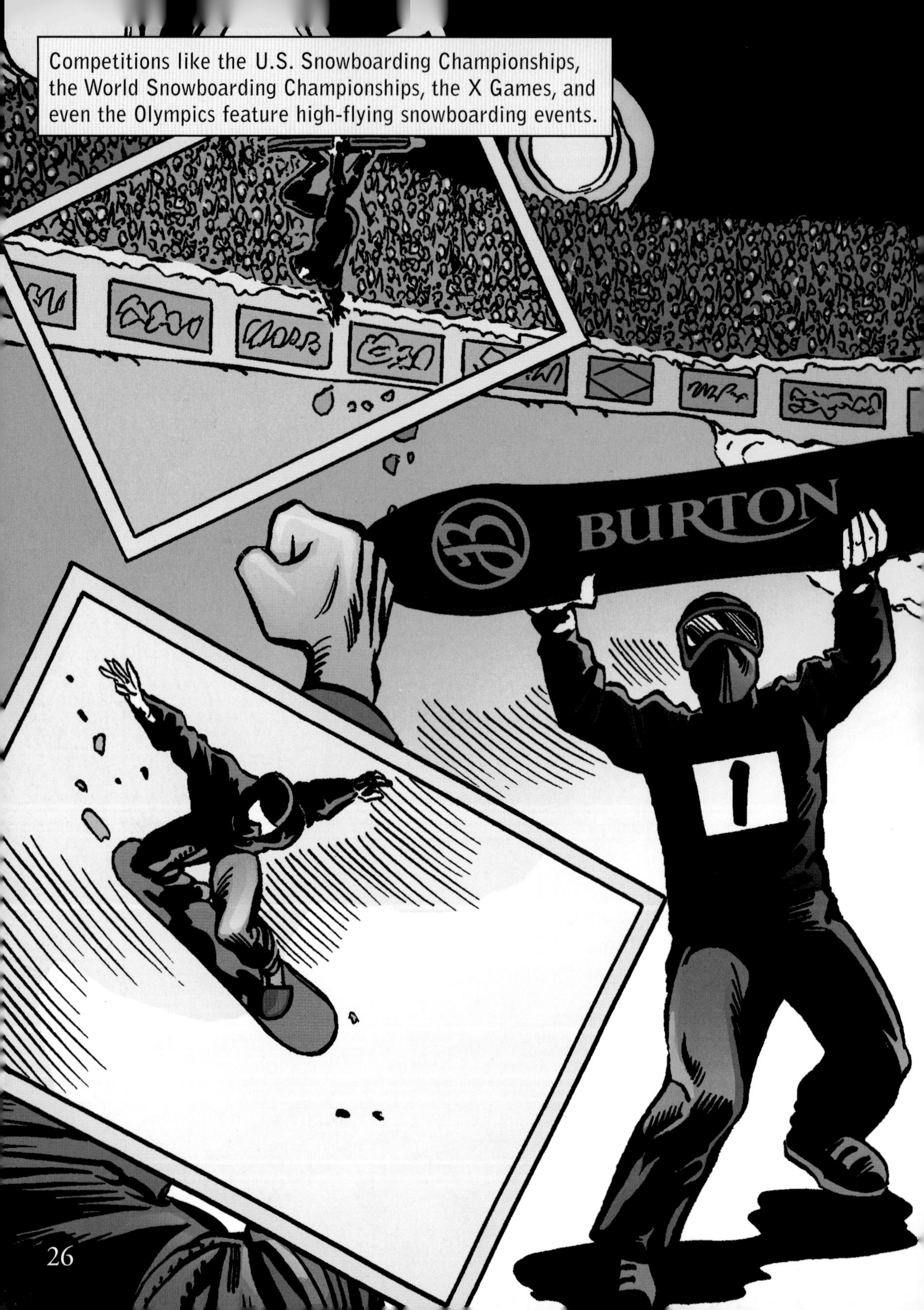
Competitions like the U.S. Snowboarding Championships, the World Snowboarding Championships, the X Games, and even the Olympics feature high-flying snowboarding events.
BURTON
1

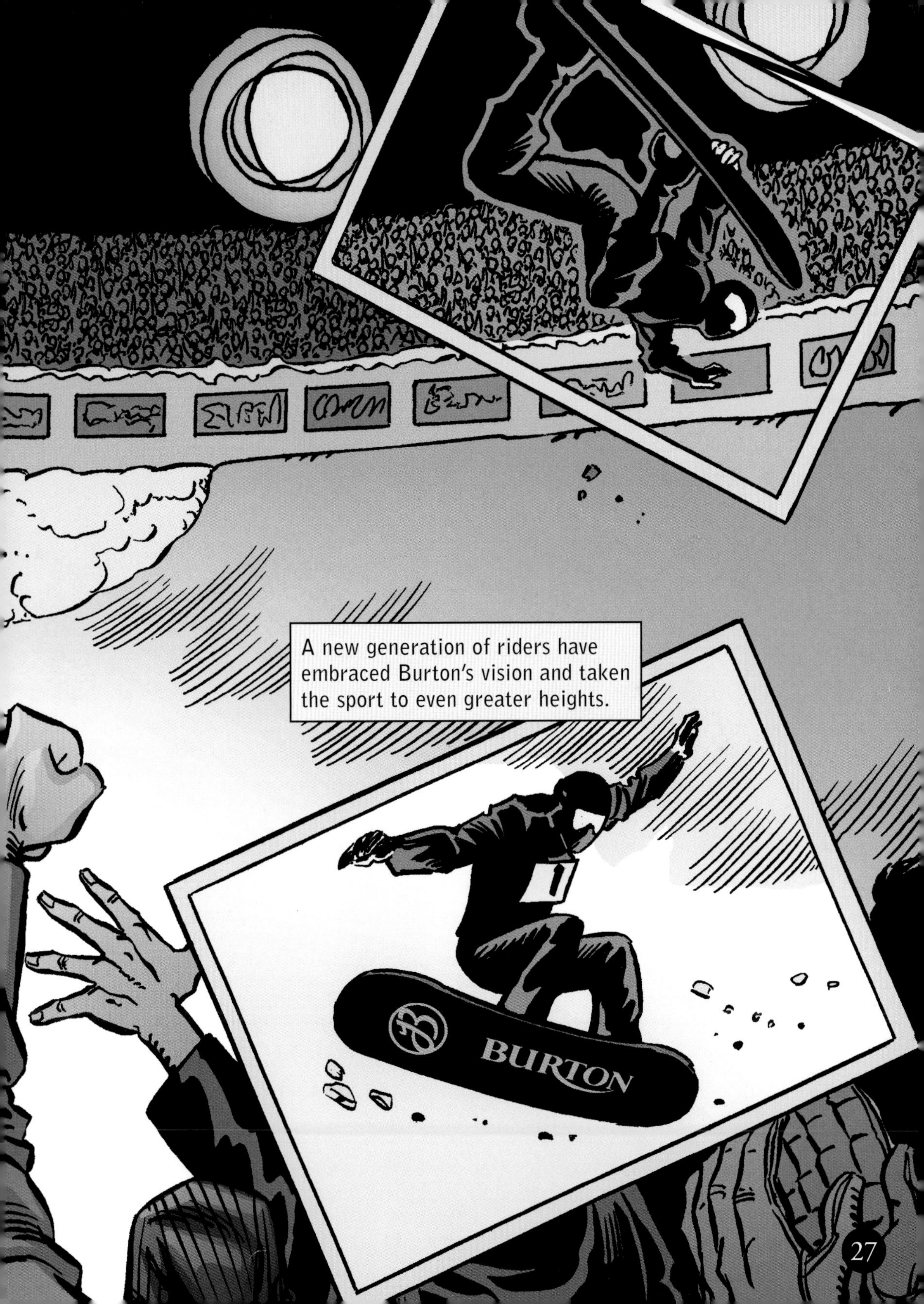
A new generation of riders have embraced Burton's vision and taken the sport to even greater heights.
1
BURTON

MORE ABOUT BURTON AND SNOWBOARDS

Jake Burton Carpenter was born in New York City, New York, on April 29, 1954. He spent most of his early years living in Cedarhurst, New York.

Jake doesn't claim to have invented the first snowboard. In fact, no one knows who did. Some believe people have been riding homemade boards since the 1920s. Others argue that a man named Vern Wicklund made the first known board. A recently discovered film shows Wicklund riding down a Chicago hill in 1939.

Most people agree that Sherman Poppen invented the first successful snowboard, called the Snurfer. On Christmas Day 1965, Poppen bound two skis together in his Muskegon, Michigan, garage. He invented the toy for his daughter but soon started selling them across the country. Eventually, Poppen sold nearly a million Snurfers.

Other snowboard pioneers include Dimitrije Milovich, Chris Sanders, Chuck Barfoot, and Tim Sims. Many of their developments made the snowboard an even better product. Milovich was the first to experiment with metal edges. He went on to create Winterstick Snowboard company. In 1985, Sims introduced the first freestyle board, which had a rounded tail.

In 1985, only 7 percent of all ski resorts allowed snowboards. But as more riders passed up backcountry powder for the ski hill snow, Jake made changes to his board. In 1980, he introduced the Performer Elite. This board was made from a special material and had metal edges to handle icy conditions.

Today, almost 8 million Americans of all ages enjoy the sport of snowboarding. Nearly every resort in the United States now welcomes these riders.

Snowboarding became an official Olympic sport at the 1998 Winter Games in Nagano, Japan. Only four years later, snowboarding was one of the most popular Olympic events. During the 2002 Olympics in Salt Lake City, Utah, thousands of fans cheered the U.S. team to a medal sweep in the halfpipe.

At the 2006 Winter Olympics, Burton Snowboards sponsored five of eight American riders, including gold medalists Shaun White and Hannah Teter.

GLOSSARY

binding (BINE-ding)—a fastening for holding the boot firmly on the snowboard

customized (KUHSS-tuh-mized)—changed to suit the needs of an individual

economics (ek-uh-NOM-iks)—the study of the way money, goods, and services are made and used in society

fiberglass (FYE-bur-glass)—a strong material made from thin threads of glass

prototype (PROH-tuh-tipe)—the first version of an invention that tests an idea to see if it will work

INTERNET SITES

FactHound offers a safe, fun way to find Internet sites related to this book. All of the sites on FactHound have been researched by our staff.

Here's how:
1. Visit *www.facthound.com*
2. Choose your grade level.
3. Type in this book ID **0736864814** for age-appropriate sites. You may also browse subjects by clicking on letters, or by clicking on pictures and words.
4. Click on the **Fetch It** button.

FactHound will fetch the best sites for you!

READ MORE

Brown, Gillian C. P. *Snowboarding*. X-treme Outdoors. New York: Children's Press, 2003.

Firestone, Mary. *Extreme Halfpipe Snowboarding Moves.* Behind the Moves. Mankato, Minn.: Capstone Press, 2004.

Gifford, Clive. *Snowboarding.* Adrenalin! North Mankato, Minn.: Chrysalis Education, 2006.

Woods, Bob. *Snowboarding.* Kids' Guides. Chanhassen, Minn.: Child's World, 2005.

BIBLIOGRAPHY

Brisick, Jamie. *Have Board, Will Travel: The Definitive History of Surf, Skate, and Snow.* New York: HarperEntertainment, 2004.

Burton Snowboards Online. http://www.burton.com

Howe, Susanna. *Sick: A Cultural History of Snowboarding.* New York: St. Martin's Griffin, 1998.

Reed, Rob. *The Way of the Snowboarder.* New York: H.N. Abrams, 2005.

INDEX